BHAGAVĀN AND BHAKTA

BHAGAVĀN AND BHAKTA

SADHVI VRINDA OM

A disciple of Om Swami

AMARYLLIS

AMARYLLIS

An imprint of Manjul Publishing House Pvt. Ltd.
• C-16, Sector 3, Noida, Uttar Pradesh 201 301, India
Website: www.manjulindia.com

Registered Office:
• 2nd Floor, Usha Preet Complex, 42 Malviya Nagar,
Bhopal 462 003 – India

Distribution Centres
Ahmedabad, Bengaluru, Chennai, Hyderabad,
Kochi, Kolkata, Mumbai, Noida, Pune

Bhagavān and Bhakta by Sadhvi Vrinda Om

First published in India by Sri Hari Press (HP) in 2024

This edition published in paperback by
Amaryllis, an imprint of Manjul Publishing House in 2025

This paperback edition first published in India in 2025
Second impression 2026

ISBN 978-93-5543-992-5

Front cover painting by R. Dukaria
Cover Design: Neelima P Aryan

Printed and bound in India by Nutech Print Services Pvt. Ltd.

THE FAIR LORD

BOOK I

(2015-2020)

A vast endless space
He has no shape
from my heart He springs
like a maddening scent from a rose.

Oh, how do I bind His kind
my mind's eye has lost Him
a zillion times
to the silliness of daytime.

O beautiful Lord, please
let love like waves rise so high
that I might drown in You
to live again.

A maddening rose, You are to me
a fragrance so pure
guileless and sure
that one day I'll surely lose my mind.

nāhaṁ prakāśaḥ sarvasya yogamāyāsamāvṛtaḥ |
mūḍho 'yaṁ nābhijānāti loko māmajamavyayam ||25||

I am not revealed to everyone, as they are veiled by My illusion (Māyā). This deluded world does not recognize Me as the unborn and the eternal.

Bhagavad Gita, 7.25.

Table of Grace

A Word of Caution

Someone once asked Swami Vivekananda if it was okay to have blind faith.

'It's fine,' Vivekananda said, 'as long as the person you have faith in is not blind.'

In the brilliance and wit of Swami Vivekananda, He probably summed up the essence of devotion. I do wonder, though, what happens when the person you believe in is a brilliant light. A light so dazzling that, no matter whether you keep your eyes open or closed, it blinds you.

That's how I find the light of my Guru Om Swami. Make no mistake, however. I don't see Him just as my guru but far beyond. At the expense of being ridiculed by those who haven't yet been transformed by Him, I see Him as an avatara. Detached, compassionate, selfless, and magical at once.

I have placed this candid admission and intention right in the beginning of the book, so whether in the free Kindle sample, or browsing in a bookstore, you may decide whether you really wish to read this book. As always, the objective is not to convince anyone. I am not the voice of reason but devotion, for it is in devotion I've had all my questions answered. It was not in reason but devotion that I found the greatest peace and joy. This is the story of Bhagavān and bhakta.

Besides, Einstein once said, 'There are only two ways to live your life. One is as though nothing is a miracle. The other is as though everything is a miracle.' When it comes to my Guru, I fall in the latter category. Everything feels unreal, it is as if it's a miracle. And so, no matter how hard I try, I am unable to contain my awe and enthusiasm. It comes out like boiling milk comes out of the saucepan. I am well aware that to many readers my writing at times may feel unctuous or even obsequious, but then again, I have not penned down this work to acquiesce the disapproving reader or please a devotee. Instead, this is a humble devotional offering at the lotus feet of my Guru.

> ***One way to think of this book is that I maintained the diary of a disciple and her inner world, and you, my dear reader, have managed to get your hands on it. No more, no less.***

I might also add that if it's in search of Bhagavān you are here, then you are in the right place. Although, it'd serve you well to have read my other works on my Guru to make complete sense of the book you hold in your hands. Regardless, these incidents spanning a decade have the power to cut through years of bleakness and darkness. To experience the extraordinary and divine presence of my Guru, it's imperative that you've done your homework before you sit down to read the most incredible life story ever written.

Other Works by Sadhvi Vrinda Om

Om Swami — As We Know Him
Book of Faith
A Prayer That Never Fails
The Rainmaker

Waking Up

Imagine you stay up and study long nights to prepare for the dreaded Math exam at the end of the academic year. All is well except one thing. You turn up at the examination centre, take your seat anxiously and the question paper says Chemistry. Chemistry? But you prepared for Mathematics. Writing this book has been something like that.

You see, it all came crashing down just when this manuscript was two weeks away from being published. I woke up that morning to face a cold, stark reality that I had written this book for all the wrong reasons. The proofreading was done, the book cover ready, e-pub merely a matter of days away, and yet, the book was all wrong.

It was all me, me and me.

There was so much of me in it that I no longer wanted anything to do with the book. I felt like I had caught my own vanity red-handed. It wasn't the splendor of my Guru that I was vocalizing. Albeit, in the guise of His truth, I was trilling my own story and in a rather shrill tone. My judgement was clouded by a subtle desire to distinguish myself. As the months passed, it had long stopped being subtle.

It was no surprise then that I now mistrusted everything that I had written, chopping off sections with a barbaric axe. The objectivity that I needed as a writer had been lost somewhere in the midst. The only saving grace was that despite my million and one flaws, being dishonest was never my thing, not for long anyway.

As the awareness came that my humble ode to my Guru, reeked of myself, I had to ask, 'Why have I written this book?'

'What was I to gain from it?'

But the answers I sought had not really come into existence. They were where they had always been – in the annals of our rich spiritual history. Swamiji's book, *The Legend of the Goddess*, had arrived at my desk for a round of editing the previous night. It was this manuscript that triggered the avalanche that crushed my work of months in one stroke. Reading through the beautiful manuscript, I came across a particular story of Chiklita Rishi as he struggled with worldly emotions and how the Divine Mother appeared to him.

> *The more Chiklita meditated on Mother Goddess's golden form, the more he wanted gold in his life which was rather strange because it was not like he had really seen the flamboyant life of Indra. But then again, he had been a witness to the affluence of Vishnu whose opulent lifestyle was vastly different to the austere one of Shiva's. What Chiklita couldn't wrap his head around was how come he had none of these desires or feelings when he left Vaikuntha. Why him, why now?*
>
> *Three years slipped by swiftly for Kardama, feeling as brief as three days, whereas for Chiklita they unfolded as if it had been a tedious span of thirty years. But their efforts*

weren't fruitless as a manifestation of Mother Goddess appeared before them.

Chiklita cried like a baby and held onto the Goddess's feet. She pulled him up and embraced him. The love and warmth she radiated soothed Chiklita's parched soul. Yes, she was the goddess of wealth and opulence, but she was also his mother and so her eyes brimmed with tears too. She understood how Chiklita had been tormented with self-doubt and desires. She didn't need him to tell her how he was torn between conflicting voices and plagued by ceaseless thoughts. She gently stroked his head and wiped a tear.

'Why mother, why?' Chiklita cried. 'Where did I go wrong?'

Upon reading of Sage Chiklita's anguish, my mind could no longer ignore where I had gone wrong. So, while I loved the Mother Goddess deeply, and just as much my Guru, my heart wasn't clear. If the learned sage was plagued by voices of wealth and power, my own mind was in the grip of a desire to make a display of the divine blessings upon me, for the whole world to see. My hard disk was corrupted by the virus of narcissism.

When the Divine Mother wiped the sage's tears, I too had cried like a baby, as if I had taken sage Chiklita's place. Reading how Mother used Her silken helm to dab the rishi's cheeks, saying She understood his torment, I had cried in relief. For just as She had appeared to absolve Her sage son, She had appeared to release me as well.

On the morning of 31st August 2023, Maa appeared as a fulsome moonbeam falling upon my face. I remember waking up at 2 am, smiling broadly as I felt Mother caressing my cheeks, my chin, as if gently waking me up with Her love. In the past too She had come at my bidding, if I had made a huge mistake, and went to bed crying for Her to set it right. As the moonlight gently fell upon my face, I felt Her gentle touch.

On waking fully though, I wasn't so sure. The recent debacle with the manuscript had hit me hard and the *Poornima*, full moon night seemed nothing more.

Two hours later, as I sat by Sri Hari's feet doing my morning japa, She came again. This time wearing a striking parrot green sari with a hint of a red-gold blouse. She sat on Her asana as Lalitambika. I wasn't calling out to Her. She sprang up in my consciousness. To find Her in the mind's eye was akin to walking into your own living room to find your Grandmother there, who lived in another country altogether.

But there wasn't much time to idle as I still had Sri Hari to dress for the day and so I parked that thought. The clock was ticking as I started dressing Sri Hari. In the little cupboard inside the sanctum sanctorum were only a handful of vastras. The chance of finding the colour I had seen Mother wearing just now was slim. But there it was the exact same shade and I pulled it out without a moment's hesitation. As I finished dressing Sri Hari and stepped back to look at Bhagavān, the ground beneath my feet shifted, She stood there very much recreated from my morning vision. It was so close to my vision that it thrilled me beyond what words can express. While dressing Her, an image of jaggery and coconut flashed in my head.

Maa wants me to make prasadam. Why?

With so many things happening within a span of four hours, as aarti finished and the calm and collected Sadhvi Nishtha was about to distribute prasadam, I asked her, a little perplexed at what was going on, 'What's so special about today's poornima?'

'Oh, it's the Rakshabandhan Poornima,' she said surprised that I didn't know.

Since, I tie Rakhi to both Lord Ganesha and Sri Hari and offer them something sweet made by my own hands, it unnerved me that I had completely forgotten about it. Just as at home the children may forget about these rituals, but a mother never does, Maa had come to remind me. I knew then that Her moon beam *sparsh*, touch, had been as real as Her appearance.

In the evening, as the Sun God climbed past the mountains, I began to doubt the morning vision again, plagued by my book's disaster. At that exact moment, a flock of parrots, flew past me, a little above my eye level, the flash of green and their red beaks unmistakable. I started laughing in disbelief.

How many more signs did I need before I believed that She had indeed come to me?

As the heavy veil of ignorance lifted, there was an overpowering need to strip away all inventions of the mind. Had this transpired fifty years earlier, my manuscript would've been torn to pieces and thrown away with no way of retrieving it, but modern gadgets provided no such satisfaction. And so, the manuscript, although mutilated, stayed on my Mac.

I began working on it all over again, examining each chapter, pressing delete, adding new sections, until I arrived at an unalloyed truth, sans the need to be seen, known or appear a certain way.

Swamiji's manuscript on the Goddess had manifested Her for me, piercing through my darkened consciousness. The vision of Mother brought in my consciousness a subtle shift. How powerful His book was going to be for times to come, I can scarcely start to imagine. But for now, dear reader, let me take you on a different journey, for this is a rare book too, it speaks of a kindness that will knead your heart into soft dough in moments and make your eyes and heart open up in unimaginable ways.

Mother Divine's shringaar based on the brief darshan in my japa on Rakshabandhan, 30th August 2023.

lelihyase grasamānaḥ samantāl lokān samagrān vadanair jvaladbhiḥ |
tejobhirāpūrya jagatsamagraṁ bhāsastavogrāḥ pratapanti viṣṇo ||

O' Viṣṇu! Devouring the worlds with Your flaming mouths, You smack Your lips on all sides. Your fiery rays, which fill the whole world with their radiance, are scorching it.

Bhagavad Gita, 11.30.

2015

Unbeknownst to Me

'The Divine Mother is present here and *ek ek taali ka hisab hoga,* every single clap will be accounted for.' With these words Swamiji left the temple, walking like a lion amidst a crowd of over two hundred people.

This was on the very first year of Sri Hari's consecration anniversary, 4th April 2015, when an all-night *jagran* (in which hymns and odes to Mother Divine were sung throughout the night) was held in the temple.

The conviction in Swamiji's voice, the truth in His words was the only anchor I had come to hold on to since the demise of my parents. Everything I knew to be true in the outside world had been based on lies told to me, by me, in the hope of leading a happier life.

He had come to be the only truth in a world made of pretense. If He had said Mother Divine was present amidst us now, then She had to be.

Throughout the night, there was beautiful roleplay of Maa's various forms, from Goddess Kali to Parvati. A couple of devotees dressed as the Goddess's lions strolled in every now and then to wake and shake people up. A glorious Lord Shiva with matted locks had also sauntered in followed by His *ganas*, demons. It was a memorable night, everyone had joined the kirtan *mandali*, musical band, in singing Maa's bhajans.

I remember sitting close to Matarani and clapping away as she sang in her beautiful, devotional voice. There's a loving quality about Swamiji's mother, one wants to be near her, to hear her voice filled with love and timeless wisdom. Only someone as pure and pious as her could have given birth to a divine being. In the temple, I knew some familiar faces, others were mere names to me, immersed in calling out to the Divine Mother. I don't remember a time when the bhajans were not playing or the clapping had come to a standstill. The temple walls reverberated with the singing and the hollering of the holy names. Happy faces were everywhere as we all sat in a semicircle singing Her praises. The night passed slowly, merrily, and at times sleepily. A few times, I rubbed my palms as they stung a bit and had turned slightly red from all the clapping.

In between, my mind would wander to Swamiji for the gift of this new life. Here I was singing kirtans when night-clubs had been more my scene just a couple of years ago, from trance to kirtan, Swamiji had been very kind to me indeed.

By 5 am, everyone was exhausted and eagerly awaited Swamiji's darshan. In His ochre robe, He glided in like a quiet sunrise showing up on the horizon and whisked away our fatigue with a sunny smile. He laughingly said He knew that quite a few had gone back to their rooms to sleep and had shown up now to see Him. His laughter filled the temple with renewed vigour. The *jagran* was concluded with Him serving the semolina halwa and *kala chana* as prasadam.

'*Sachiyan jyota wali mata, teri sada hi jai. Bolo sanche darbar ki jai,*' the beautiful *jaikara* in Swamiji's voice sounded like a promise of great things to come.

The day after, when I met him, He said to me, 'I was telling Matarani and a few others how you never stopped clapping that night.'

I looked at Him in amazement, 'Really, I never stopped clapping, uh I don't think I remember, Swamiji.'

'Yes, you clapped the entire night, never stopping.'

'Whole night, really, I did that?'

I was really perplexed. All I remembered was that each time I had thought of resting my hands in my lap, I had joined them back instantly remembering what Swamiji had said about the Divine Mother's sacred presence in the temple, and I didn't wish to disrespect Her.

Still, I wondered how He knew. In the early days, Swamiji would sometimes say that He spoke to the Divine Mother but in the later years Swamiji stopped making those references altogether. And so, I thought maybe Maa had told Him. My mind was whirring like a fan on full speed but still I couldn't make sense of it.

Swamiji's smile grew a little wider as He had said,

'Not only did you clap the whole night, but you were also the only one who did.' The look on His face as if I had done Him proud was so new to me that I wished that I could always make Him proud. Besides, now I was even more zapped that He had an account not merely of me but of everyone present there.

How could He know sitting in His cottage what two hundred people had been up to? And what about the blessing?

A faint smile played on Swamiji's lips as He read my mind, 'All in good time.'

The Sacred Aarti

H*aath aao toh butt, haath na aao toh khuda ho…* If anyone can hold you, you are merely an idol and if they can't reach you, you are God, is a Sufi saying I've heard from Swamiji a few times in His discourses. The descent of Bhagavān in the consciousness of a devotee takes time. Until it seeps in, all idols and statues appear just that – statues. Whereas once you have fallen in devotion, the same idol becomes your ideal. You begin to see how Chaitanya Mahaprabhu or Mirabai felt what they had when it came to Lord Jagannath and Dwarikadhish Sri Krishna, respectively.

When I first began to do Sri Hari's aarti in the sanctum sanctorum, it was no more than a daily ritual to me. I'd hold the lamp high up to His face. The shadow from the flame of five wicks would cast a beautiful fiery reflection in His eyes, creating a magical moment in which Bhagavān's eyes seemed to be watching me. There are billions of people like me who want to feel special, that we matter to at least someone in this world. And in that moment standing next to the Lord, it felt like I did matter to Him.

After my turn was over and I had handed the aarti to the next in line, I'd stand in a corner, close my eyes and try to feel His presence, to experience a little of the love my Guru felt for Sri Hari. How He never took His eyes off Bhagavān's face and sang to Him as one sings to a real person, with great depth of feelings and emotion.

Unfortunately, my mind would be everywhere other than where I was. Those ten minutes of aarti felt the longest. Sometimes, the people standing nearby would be a source of irritation and at times those far away. All this and more went on in my head just when the aarti was going on. It seemed like there was no way to silence the mind just when I needed it to be quiet. It was a beautiful eulogy penned by Swamiji to propitiate Sri Hari and it deserved every bit of my attention. The divine hymn was sung each morning and evening, and to fight my wandering mind, I began to practice visualization of the stanzas, like a story unfolding in my mind's eye.

I'd imagine Lord Hari dark as the blue night, His eyes deep pools of laughter and kindness, resting in the milky ocean of bliss. Bhagavān's long and delicate feet nestled in Mahalakshmi's lap. She was as fair and pink as He was dark and dazzling. I could never decide whether the Divine Mother was dressed in pink or in red. Years later, I found the perfect bright pink of the wild rose variety that I thought was the colour that suited Her the most.

The gentle lapping of the waves made the most serene sound, as the divine couple reposed in the middle of the ocean. In my imagination, far away on a silver shore, I stood stranded, a mere child of five, desperately trying to find my way to them.

Sometimes, I'd beg Lord Garuda, Bhagavān's mount to drop me in the sea, close to the coiled serpent. And from there I'd begin my steep climb to the holy feet of the Divine Mother. Always to Her auspicious feet first, as I had heard Swamiji say time and again that without Her blessings one couldn't hope to find Bhagavān. There was a more pressing reason though, the most important one being - She was the Mother whose love I anxiously sought. Hiding behind Her feet, in the folds of Her sari, dozing off was one of my most coveted things. In my universe, She always had time for me.

In one version of my visualization, we'd wait up for Bhagavān to return from running a billion galaxies. And as any parent does, He'd make a beeline for Maa and me, tuck me in before I went to sleep. To me it was important that Maa and Bhagavān were always together. In all the years, I could never imagine Her without Bhagavān or Him without Her, for then my illusion would break.

It'd be yet another dysfunctional family like the one I had. In my mind's eye, they were always together, and I a little child snuggled right between them.

For so long this thought brought me such comfort that every day I returned to this place, to feel loved and safe. Whether it was my *japa*, chanting or aarti, the early years of my sannyasa had more or less similar visualizations. It's been seven years and the aarti is my *nitya* karma, daily spiritual practice, without fail, no matter where I am or how I am doing.

But there's more to this story, as there usually is. This love for aarti was quite the reverse once. The polar opposite, in fact. It began with a dreadful incident in December 2015. It was a cold December evening in the ashram and 4.30 pm on the clock. It was my turn to make the evening meal for Swamiji. For some reason, of which I have no recollection now, I was, at the time, terribly upset. It happened a lot back then, as I was deeply scarred and wounded inside.

I stood at the door to Swamiji' study and said to Him that I was in no state to make a meal, let alone serve it. His calm gaze settled on my face, and it was a moment before He spoke, 'Sure, Dolly, you don't have to make it, if you aren't feeling well, Vidya Swami will do it.'

I kept standing there not knowing what to do. I felt bad for backing out at the last minute.

'I always offer the first morsel to the Divine Mother. To serve Her food cooked in a disturbed or negative state of mind is never my preference.'

I gave in then. Swamiji had always known what would make me alright and His advice was the only one I ever paid heed to, so I asked Him how to make myself okay.

'Please go attend the evening aarti and you'll feel better,' He said smilingly.

'Is it going to make any difference, Swamiji, it's the same aarti, I sing every day,' I flippantly added, 'It's repetitive and boring.'

A long silence ensued, in which it felt as if every particle, every atom surrounding Swamiji had frozen in time. I thought He was angry with me, but as I observed His face keenly, I realized that I had wounded Him deeply with my words. He had always been so kind and gentle to me that I felt a tight knot in my heart at hurting the one person who cared about my existence.

I mumbled a hasty apology saying that I'll indeed attend the aarti. With a heart heavy as a brick, I took an evening shower and went to the temple. While everyone sang the aarti, I merely mouthed the words with tears flowing down my face. I felt so small and selfish. I cried sorry tears, all for me, neither Bhagavān nor anyone else mattered at the time. I had wondered then if there'll ever come a time when I'll cry for Him as intensely as I cried for myself.

I must have slept late that night, as I had made no morning plans to attend the aarti again. It hadn't brought me any peace the previous evening and so, I thought it best to give it a pass. As I slept that night, somewhat sad and weary, I saw Sri Hari. The beautiful black *vigraha*, had magically appeared in my head. It felt insane, to have Him looking at me, from inside me.

I can't really explain it, but let me try with an example. It was just like someone leaning forward from a balcony to look at a person standing below. Sri Hari was leaning into my mind, while He stood perfectly still in the Sanctum Sanctorum. It's the best I can do; all I know is that He was inside my head, staring at me with His laughing eyes. His face was inches away from mine, as He playfully said, '*Meri aarti nahi gaogi*, Dolly, will you not sing my aarti.'

I wondered if He was real or I was dreaming. The next moment there was a blinding flash to Bhagavān's right. His *Sudarshan* chakra, the discus, was whirring so fast that it terrified me. The dazzling light from the whizzing discus had burst into my mind, like an explosion from a bomb. The bright and luminous light jolted me out of sleep as I sat up in bed, hands joined above my head, mumbling, '*Main gaongi main gaongi,* I will sing, I will sing your aarti.' Bhagavān smiled widely as I had said that, and then, He was gone just like that.

I looked outside, and the sun was shining bright. The clock by my bedside read 6 am. I shakily tried to make sense of my dream. *Sri Hari had come to call me for the aarti.*

A little awed, a lot more scared, I got ready for the temple for the 7 am aarti. The golden daze, the whirring of the blazing discus had intimidated me more than anything. To dream of Bhagavān's face was one thing but to be woken up with a mythical weapon moving faster than the speed of light was another. It wasn't my imagination. It was real and truly scary, for not only did Bhagavān exist, His *ayudha*, weapons, were just as real. I was both thrilled and terrified at the same time.

As soon as it was feasible, I made my way to Swamiji's study. This time with great humility and an appetizing lunch tray in hand. He had barely eaten a few bites when I blurted out what had happened. I didn't have the patience to wait for Him to finish His meal. A big smile appeared on His face as He put a spoonful of rice in His mouth.

'Swamiji, how could Sri Hari be inside my head?'

'You didn't believe He was real, Dolly, so Bhagavān came to give you a little peak of His grandeur.'

Today, as I'm a bit wiser, I see this incident in a different light. All the religious fanaticism and rigidity in the world in the name of God seems so useless. For Bhagavān, the Parabrahma, has only love in His heart even for the one who thinks His rituals boring. There's no wrathful God out there. He's the gentlest, kindest and most playful entity to whom the whole universe belongs. Even in His command to attend the aarti, there was a loving humor. He didn't hold my ignorance against me, instead, offered a chance to find Him. That He should appear in jest for a tiny person like me, who had never really prayed to Him in her life, was stupefying.

It raised more questions in me than answers, whom had I stumbled upon and what was I to do now? I had nothing to offer Him, beyond a repertoire of two-three recently learnt bhajans. In fact, I'd sing the same bhajans every day in the temple, more than once sometimes.

A few days after Bhagavān's dream, Swamiji laughingly said to me, 'Maybe you should learn more bhajans, mix it with a little harmonium, it'd be a nice change for Sri Hari to hear something new.'

It was really hilarious because I had never told Swamiji that I knew very few bhajans. And that I had been bellowing in Sri Hari's ears every day. After Swamiji, cracked that joke, Vidya Swami started to tease me and said, 'Do you know where Bhagavān goes when you are singing in the temple?'

I shook my head as I didn't really get his question.

'Bhagavān is out pacing in the garden, for if He had to hear the same bhajan once more He'd run away.'

api cetsudurācāro bhajate māmananyabhāk |
sādhureva sa mantavyaḥ samyagvyavasito hi saḥ ||30||
kṣipraṁ bhavati dharmātmā śaśhvacchāntiṁ nigacchhati |
kaunteya pratijānīhi na me bhaktaḥ praṇaśyati ||31||

Even if the most immoral person worships Me with unwavering devotion, such a person must be considered saintly, as he becomes righteous. Swiftly, he becomes virtuous and attains everlasting peace. O' Kaunteya, I declare boldly that My Bhakta (devotee) never perishes.

Bhagavad Gita, 9.30–31.

2016

The Flow Called Life

Three months had passed since Sri Hari had appeared with a discus in hand. After the initial elation wore off, I forgot what was expected of me. As life would have it, I started to experience symptoms of acute sadness and intense melancholy once again. It invariably led to a feeling of ending my life and mulling over ways to end it. The exasperation of not being able to go through with it, the worthlessness of life, built-up in my head, like a musical crescendo driving me mad. My life had no purpose, no meaning, no family and certainly no reason to want to live.

On 25th March 2016, angry at myself, I vowed to sing the aarti every day thinking maybe it'd help calm my mind as Swamiji had said. I had to at least try. A week later I visited the ashram and the rewards of obeying Bhagavān's command to sing the aarti were there for me to see.

During the morning Abhishekam of 4th April, the consecration anniversary, the Vishnu Sahasranama was being chanted as milk, yogurt and honey were generously poured to anoint

Bhagavān's beautiful dark form. My tears matched every ingredient drop by drop as I cried miserably from being mentally sad and utterly lonely. I kept saying to Sri Hari, 'Call me to you, call me to you, please, I just don't want to live.'

The more I cried, it seemed the more He smiled, as if saying, *you know that's not happening.* It actually felt like I was talking to a stone. In extreme agony, I said to Him, *Fine, if you won't call me to You, then give me something to do with my life. Give me sannyasa, what else is left for me to do.*

The minute these words were out there, I had experienced great shock. *Had I really asked Bhagavān for sannyasa?*

When the Abhishekam had begun, I was a crying trembling mess, twenty-five minutes later I sat there unsure of what I had just asked Bhagavān for. These were not my words. I had always resisted the idea of sannyasa.

In 2014, when I had the vision of Swamiji in his astral form and saw my soul in an ochre hue, I had dismissed it as a dream (I've written about it in *Om Swami As We Know Him*). I had so many desires in me that I, more than anyone, knew were most ill-suited to be a sannyasi. I had no desire to be one.

To add to that, I had recently spent a small fortune sprucing up my wardrobe with winter-wear from Zara, Mango and other brands to keep myself cozy in the ashram winter. The thought that I could no longer wear them was a hugely disturbing factor. Yes, I know that sounds downright stupid, but that was me. In reality, my clothes, my thinking, my speech, my life thus far, were all wrong for this vocation. I was a silly person at times and even I knew that.

And yet, here in a moment, Sri Hari had wrangled out of me an admission that was the furthest from my mind. To me it was an equivalent of giving up my life and everything I held dear. It was dying. As a reader, you might think that I'm being delusional when I say that but, somewhere Bhagavān had made me ask Him for sannyasa. He had. Even though I had mouthed those words, He was the one who had supplanted and supplied them. My mind was so unsure of what had just happened and why I would ask for something that I had never wanted in the first place.

Swamiji, the omniscient, all-knowing force alone knows, it is the truth. It was as if the Divine had been waiting all this while for me to admit, accept defeat. I was indeed defeated, by my desires, all that sadness lumped inside that wouldn't let me lead a normal, sane life.

I rushed to Swamiji to offer my pranams and as soon as His breakfast was over, I looked towards Him. With my face still tear-stained, I said, 'Swamiji, please give me sannyasa.'

I hadn't expected Swamiji to start laughing, 'You want sannyasa now. This is quite a development.'

Oh, how beautifully He laughs, flawless in every way, from the tone of His fair skin to the gentle tone of His speech. A decade in His service and His laughter leaves me speechless even today. I repeated my request.

'What has brought on this change of heart?' He said.

Emboldened because He hadn't rejected the idea outright, I narrated the morning's mental conversation with Sri Hari.

'Fine, think it over, let some time pass and we'll revisit this.'

He didn't reject my plea outright and that in itself was an achievement as far as I was concerned. The next few weeks were spent finalizing the edits of *Om Swami As We Know Him*. Harper Collins had scheduled the book to be released in July.

The book still carries my old name as an author, for until April I didn't know that I was going to be a sannyasi. But Swamiji knew. Here's a passage from the book where Swamiji had predicted in March 2014 what went on to unfold in 2016.

> *'Swami, what about me? There were two of me. I was coloured ochre, the colour of your robe. Is that how our auras look?'*
>
> *'No, they really have no colour.'*
>
> *'Then why did I look all ochre?'*
>
> *'It's the colour of devotion, of surrender, just like Mira loved Girdhar Gopal …'*
>
> *'You saw two of you,' He continued. 'One is who you are currently. And the second is who you will be in the future. This is the path of transformation. Only the dye of devotion will wash off the various colours of grief, desires and pain I see in you. Ochre is the colour of surrender, of devotion. It's the colour of the rising sun, of the setting sun; it's the colour of fire. All your afflictions will burn and the real you will shine forth. It'll take time, but it'll happen, Dolly.'*

Seven years and three months to this day, the battle to fight these afflictions is still on. Though, I've come far, but longer still is the road that lies ahead. It'd be clichéd to quote Robert Frost, but he alone comes to mind.

> *The woods are lovely, dark, and deep*
> *But I have promises to keep,*
> *And miles to go before I sleep,*
> *And miles to go before I sleep.*

The Gift of Sannyasa

Swamiji looked so tranquil seated on His asana, the twin *tilakams* on His forehead shining. Every auspiciousness seemed to surround him. There was not a single hurried movement. His *tapas* like a powerful beam of light, radiated from Him a warmth, a quiet power that had no explanation in human terms. He was, in that moment, an entity whose power spilled out as gentle radiance in the morning air.

Kneeling in front of Swamiji, as He chanted a mantra, His thumb on my forehead, I was filled with joy and trepidation. He wasn't smiling, His eyes were solemn as mine were filled with anticipation. It was 6 am and the solemn ceremony of initiation had just begun.

Mellifluous Sanskrit verses flowed out of Him like lightening in the sky. I was too stunned to remember much except that a single tear rolled down my cheek when He had said, *'From this day on Parmeshawara, the Lord Narayana has accepted you. You belong to Him now.'*

To this day the only line I remember is that Bhagavān had accepted me.

All the struggles in life had been to belong, and here in one moment Swamiji had given me eons of blessings. On the Guru Purnima of 19th July 2016, I was initiated into sannyasa by Swamiji.

'Your Guru mantra I've given you after careful consideration. It's one of my awakened mantras. In time, it'll help you heal and bless people.'

I could only gape at Him. Little did I know that His magnanimity was boundless, and He had just begun giving.

'Go, Sadhvi Vrinda and give up your life in the service of mankind.'

There couldn't have been enough gratitude in my heart to stand in front of His pristine presence, nor can there ever be. Even if I'm buried a thousand times, and I take rebirth, I shall not be able to repay His kindness at all.

I came out dazed. The beautiful Navjot Gautam and Vidya Swami waited for me in the kitchen. Nav had lovingly cooked the sweet *kadah prasadam*, so I could offer it to Swamiji on the conclusion of my initiation. When I offered it to Swamiji, He ate exactly three spoonfuls, 'One each for Brahma, Vishnu and Mahesh.'

Matarani, Swamiji's darling mother, and adorable elder sister, Didi, were also eagerly waiting outside the cottage. They had each brought exquisite gold earrings as gifts. These gifts, I knew, were there because there were no parents or family members waiting for me. From the first moment on, they have always strived to make me feel that I'm not alone in this world.

Swamiji and His family, I dare say, are like His reflection; His feelings are often reflected in the gestures of Matarani and Didi.

I see it so clearly. In that moment, my puny heart was so full as I fluttered about as a butterfly gathering fragrant and sweet gifts from every direction. The day was far from over, in the evening, when Swamiji went up for the Guru Purnima celebration, I had no idea that I'd soon be crying like a child at His divine feet. I've pulled out some passages from the video recording of the evening discourse by Swamiji on 19th July 2016.

> *'It's a beautiful day today, and if the children are being noisy, just bring them to me here in front, and we'll have their discourse first!' The audience burst into laughter as Swamiji looking radiant in black began the discourse.*
>
> *'It's easy with them,' He continued, 'And that's because a child's language is simple, and devoid of pretense. This is the reason childlike people always reach God quicker. Those with simple, innocent hearts, reach the divine with ease as compared to those who are very intelligent, or clever. The ones who possess great intellect and lots of knowledge find it harder to reach God, because while it can be a means to the divine, it can also become an obstacle on the spiritual path. When we do Sadhana one of the reasons why we completely go down to the root level is to destroy our ego and the delusion that we know a lot.'*
>
> *It is believed that when somebody leaves this world, they cannot return. At least not in the same body. A person who departs this world, never really comes back to it. A person who is dead, is dead. And when somebody loses their parents, one who loses their mother or father, they can never return to this world no matter how much you pray or want them to come back. No amount of intense desire for their return amounts to anything. No matter how excellent your*

samskaras, or the amount of penance you may have and spiritual wealth you may have accumulated, nothing can bring them back. However, there is one loophole, there is one path which can bring your mother and father back into your life. So, today is the day of Sadhvi Vrinda Om's initiation. Please come here Sadhviji, I'm going to put my hand on your head.

'Sadhvi Vrinda Om, from this moment on, you are not an orphan, Swami is your father and your mother. I will, and in front of Sri Hari I'm saying this, I will make you a healer par excellence. I will give you both, Sadhana and Siddhis...'

'Her heart is pure, I can see that, irrespective of whether others can see it or not. Sadhviji, your blessings will bear fruit.'

I always say there are two things nobody can really give you. Perhaps at someone's behest you may momentarily be given these, but in most cases, you must earn these two things and those are, first, love, and second, respect.

You earn love and respect based on the merit of your own actions and nobody can give these to you. However, it is only in a culture as beautiful as the Indian culture and a dharma as unique as Sanatana Dharma, where saints are revered deeply. The reverence we hold for the ochre robe of a sannyasi and the amazing fact of how people can derive so much strength and divinity just from this robe. Not the ones who are donning it, which is a separate matter, it's the ones who go looking for them.'

What is so special about Indian culture and Sanatana Dharma is the aspect of the sacred Guru–Shishya tradition. This tradition (Parampara) has been carried down through millions and billions of years.

For one who has been initiated into Sannyasa, and dons the ochre robe; whomsoever approaches them with a devotional, humble sentiment, (with bhava) or a true desire in their hearts, is not turned away. However, the blessing is not given by their physical bodies. For instance, Vidya Swami has a wealth of his own sadhana, if he blesses somebody, he will have to take it out of his sadhana and give it to the one who seeks it. And more importantly when somebody blesses another in these robes, there is the power of all those hundreds and thousands of sages connected over eons and ages. That entire lineage of siddhas and their blessings get connected to them, and they all empower the word of a saint, provided the saint is properly initiated into the right lineage.

I had once heard a beautiful story in Uttar Pradesh.

There was a young woman who went to visit a renowned astrologer in ancient India, one who was known to be an ardent devotee of Lord Rama. It is said that this was Goswami Tulsidas himself.

She went to Goswami Tulsidas seeking his counsel and confided in him that she had no children yet and she desperately wanted a child. Goswami ji had his trustworthy Prashnawali with him. There is one that is found in the Ramcharitmanas and there's another one which has 108 shlokas (verses) and after the meaning of every shloka there is a siddhi mentioned after that.

Goswami had his own fool proof way of asking Bhagavān Rama any question from the Prashnawali and getting exact answers from it. So, he posed the woman's problem as a question to Lord Rama and the Lord replied clearly through the Prashnawali (questionnaire) that she had no 'yoga' for a child in her destiny, it just wasn't written in the stars.

As was the case, Goswami Tulsidas delivered the message to her, as it is. He told her that Lord Rama had Himself in no uncertain terms said that she couldn't have a child.

She retorted, 'Can't your Lord Rama do anything then? The Lord of all the worlds can't do anything to help me?'

Goswami ji replied, 'Please know that the answers from my Lord's Prashnawali never lie, I am simply telling you what's written, because beyond this I don't know anything.'

There was another saint in those times, a contemporary of Goswami Tulsidas, who the lady went to visit next with her plea. She expressed her deep desire to have a child in his presence and baba, the saint, pleased with her, instantly blessed her and said, 'Go now, don't you worry, you shall have a son. I'm pleased with your prasad.' She had taken some laddoos for the saint, just for the record and he was so pleased with her offering that without giving it a second thought he gave her a blessing that she would definitely have a son. Indeed, nine months later the lady gave birth to a baby boy, and not only that, the year after, she was also blessed with another child, this time a daughter.

The woman felt the joy and fulfilment of a complete family and decided to visit Goswami Tulsidas again, taking both her children along with her. Goswami recognized the lady from afar and remembered her clearly and why she had come to see him two years earlier. What amazed him, though, were the children she was carrying in her arms, and he asked her outright, 'I remember you, but please tell me whose kids are you carrying with you?'

She replied, 'Maharaj, they are my children.'

Goswami shook his head in disbelief and said, 'That is impossible, the Prashnawali is the word of my Lord Rama, its answers, its shloka and chaupaiyan can never be false. I don't believe you; you are testing me, these cannot be your children.'

'No baba, these are in fact my children. Just after I met you that day, and you said that your Lord Rama says I cannot have children, I visited this other baba's ashram and now with the power of his blessings, I have two children.'

Goswami was shocked to hear how that could have even been possible. He thought about how when he had delivered the word of the Prashnawali, he had no selfish motive attached to it, and so then there was no reason why his word should go false and, more importantly, there was no plausible reason as to why His Lord's word could go false.

So, a very distraught and sad Goswami left the woman outside and sat at his place of worship near the altar. He called out to his Lord Rama with great fervour. He cried out desperately to the Lord, 'Prabhu, today you must give me some answers, you have to come to me. You must tell me how this is even possible, because I do not care about my word one bit, but if your word goes false, then what is left? Where will people go? They will stop believing in Dharma.'

As he was crying and repeatedly calling the Lord's name, he fell asleep on his asana and in a dream, Lord

Rama appeared, and a conversation ensued between Bhagavān and his bhakta.

Goswami said, 'Hey Raghunath, what is this leela? What is this play of yours? From your own Prashnawali you clearly told me that this lady could not have a child. It wasn't in her destiny and then you gave her two children. I don't understand this at all.'

Bhagavān replied, 'Tulsidas, there is an ardent devotee of mine, a yogi, who has such deep faith in the power of his devotion to me, in the power of his sadhana and penance, that he did not think it necessary to ask me before blessing that woman. He simply gave his word with conviction in his heart, that she would have children. How could I not honour my own devotee's word? It is alright if my word goes false through the Prashnawali, but his word could not have proved false. He trusted me with all his heart, and based on unwavering faith that I, his Lord Rama, would never let his word be false or an empty one.'

The name of that saint was Baba Kinnaram. Even to this day, his ashram exists in UP.

So, a sannyasi should either have done a lot of penance or have a pure heart, and if she/he has both, well then that's a deadly combination. If a sannyasi is pure at heart and has also done sadhana, then there is nothing more one can have or acquire, to help and benefit other people.

When such a person gives his or her word, or rather when such a 'vibhuti' entity, blesses other people, it holds water and comes to fruition sooner or later, that word does not go false.

The human mind, though, thinks very differently. A human being thinks, I want something, and I want it now within this timeframe. If I get it within the frame I've decided, then its good otherwise all of this is meaningless.

However, if not in this lifetime, then that wish does certainly get fulfilled in another lifetime. You would have to return for the fulfillment of that wish, because a blessing of a saint is attached to it. Just because of that one desire and fulfilment of that word, you may have to come back, because nature always operates on its own time scale. Which is why one should be very careful about what they wish for and ask for from anyone, especially Bhagavān.

You should think hard before you ask for things, because that may be the only reason why most of you are on this planet Earth today. It's because of the things you wanted in your previous lifetimes and you're getting some of those fulfilled now.

Nature moves at its own pace, like if you board a train, no matter how rushed you may be, you may even be the Prime Minister of the country and have contacts and know the driver but even then, he can't make it go any faster, the train will go at its own pace. Similarly, everybody here, each one of us, are all aboard the train of nature and it will move at its own pace. Nature absolutely does not care about individual temperaments or preferences. It has no prejudice. Whatever life gives you, if you accept it gracefully, gratefully, happily and even willingly, then you make your own life easier. However, if you resist and battle with yourself and life, nothing will come of it, except suffering.

I started crying when Swamiji had announced that I wasn't an orphan anymore. I had cried even more when He had spoken of making me a healer par excellence. I alone knew my own unreadiness, unworthiness and un-deservingness that evening and yet, Swamiji's blessings were infinite.

After the discourse, when Swamiji beckoned me to attend the aarti, I was given the *Chanwar*, a fan to wave for Bhagavān. My hands had trembled, as big fat tears had threatened to roll over. Through a haze of tears, I gazed at my Guru, as He sang the aarti...He was all light, brilliant and white, His gaze fixed at Sri Hari, as if engaged in silent conversation with Him.

Before we go any further, I'm reminded of this time when Swamiji once told Vidya Swami and I that during Bhagavān's aarti, his mind is completely thoughtless. No matter what, there's not another person, another thought in his mind except Bhagavān in that moment.

In the earlier years, when Swamiji used to do Hare Krishna kirtans in the temple on certain occasions, He would, to the surprise of all present, sometimes drape the head dress around His neck on Bhagavān's dark shoulders. I'd bothered Swamiji by asking a few times as to why He did so, but He had always smiled my curiosity away. This one time, as Bhagavān's grace would have it, Swamiji was listening to a Vishnu *stuti* and was in a mellowed devotional sentiment. I chose that moment to humbly ask Him about the mystery behind the headcover.

It turned out that when Bhagavān had appeared before Him on 11th May 2011, much had transpired which our Guru has always shied away from sharing. It'd take Him into a trance from where there was no returning. But what He did tell me, though, was that during the vision that had lasted hours, Bhagavān had playfully taken away Swamiji's head cover.

Later, as Swamiji had come out of the vision, the head cover was no longer on Him. It's why, out of deep love, Swamiji would sometimes offer His head cover to the Absolute Being the controller of everything in existence. To hear that Bhagavān, the absolute power in the universe, is so playful and loving is like a shock at first because, all our lives, we've either mostly feared Him or prayed to Him out of desperation. But seeing Swamiji, hearing Him speak, there remains no doubt in one's mind that this is how Bhagavān must be, ever kind, ever loving and ever filled with laughter and kind mischief.

A Powerful Lineage

The next morning, I was to leave for the city in my ochre robes for the very first time. I went to take my leave from Swamiji; as a disciple, there was now a greater accountability to uphold protocol. As I entered the study, my eyes fell straight on the side table that had a parcel on it. It was wrapped in white cotton cloth, embroidered with bright red thread, giving it an Assamese make.

For some strange reason that I just couldn't fathom, I was deeply pulled towards it.

'Swamiji, what is that?' I said avidly, eyeing the white cloth in the corner. I knew fully well that I could no longer hope to wear it, but my heart was somehow set on it. I started walking in its direction, like one goes after a mythical golden creature, well before Swamiji had called out from the end of His long study, 'Bring it to me.'

A mischievous smile played on His lips as He carefully unwrapped the white cloth and lo and behold, beneath the white cotton was a red cloth in pure silk. On one corner of it was written, *for the Governor of Assam*.

'It seems this has come for you,' Swamiji said, handing it over to me.

Smiling like a child, Swamiji explained that in yesterday's meeting, a lady had brought this as a gift for Him. It was a sari the Mother Divine had worn in the Kamakhya temple, in Assam. The lady was touching 70 years of age and she didn't know how much longer she could look after the sacred cloth.

As soon as I heard this, I knew that something was pulling me to that parcel in the corner. The energy of Maa's Sari had created such an acute desire in me to possess it that I had nearly snatched it myself. In the later years, all my Devi sadhanas were done with that Sari draped around my shoulders.

Upon returning from the ashram, I felt the need to have a simple *nitya*-pooja, daily-worship routine. Swamiji, in His practical way, had advised me to do one round of Guru mantra every day, which would suffice as the *nitya* pooja. This had sounded too simple, even for me.

'Surely, there's more to it, Swamiji. You used to chant for such long hours, and I just have to do one round of the beads?'

'In due course, you'll do proper sadhanas and then you can do longer hours.'

I was about to take His leave when He said, 'You know, you must read the Tulasi Ramayana, it'll evoke sentiments of devotion in you.'

Ah devotion, I thought, I definitely needed loads of it. All the rewards had been given, now was the time to earn them. As a new sannyasi, I wanted to do so much more but Swamiji's instructions were simple: one round of Guru-mantra and Ram-charitmanas daily. I started these practices right away. I knew so little about Sanatana Dharma. No one in our family had known much, except my mother, who was more of an intuitive worshiper than anything else. I had the desire to worship, but the knowledge and know-how were zilch.

It then occurred to me that Sri Hari Himself had asked me to do His aarti, so why didn't I start it already? Plus, I found the piano version of the aarti by Swamiji quite enjoyable. So, one day, I sat down and made myself a *nitya*-pooja routine.

Beginning with the aarti, followed by the Srividya *stuti*, hymn, and finishing with a round of the Guru mantra. This simple pooja routine of twenty minutes in the next seven years would grow to two hours. But of course, back then, it was inconceivable to me.

On day one, I knelt on the ground to offer my obeisance to a small *vigraha* of Goddess Durga made of clay. It had been with me for four years, the toughest four years. I had an affinity to Bhagavān but never had anything special really happen before that day.

Kneeling on the floor, I sang the Srividya *stuti* hoping to capture Swamiji's tone and inflections. In the middle of the *stuti*, a beautiful woman, for want of a better expression, posed as a traditional Kathak dancer appeared before my mind's eye. She wore bright silk garments, with gold chokers around her neck, arms and wrists, and there was a simple gold crown on her head. Her big red bindi, dazzling ornaments and the red and gold of her dress made me think that she was attractive but not stunning enough to be the Divine Mother.

Her unblinking eyes weren't hostile, but they weren't friendly either. For a moment, my heart lurched, thinking that maybe I had done something wrong. I even tried to shake her out of my head, but her image stayed, like a painting on a wall. Quickly completing the *stuti*, I placed my head on the ground. As soon as I stopped singing, she was gone. I got through the next twenty minutes of the aarti and the japa a little disturbed. The first day of my *nitya*-pooja hadn't turned out to be as serene as I had hoped it'd be. I was scared.

I get scared quite easily, so I emailed Swamiji asking if I had made some mistake in my practice. He, who knows everything, replied that since I was a part of the lineage now, when I had done Devi Maa's *stuti*, one of Her companion energies from a retinue of sixty-four came to see who was calling out to the Mother Divine. When later I met Swamiji in the ashram, He jokingly said, 'She came to check on you, wondering who's this petulant child calling out to the Mother Goddess.'

As my love and worship of the Divine Mother grew over the years, Swamiji had an insightful observation to share.

From my mother's side, we were Kashyaps, and her Kul Devi had always been Maa Durga. As I walked on the spiritual path, my inclination to worship the Kul Devi of my ancestors had rekindled. I had no prior knowledge of this until Swamiji had pointed out how my natural inclination was always to run and pray to the Divine Mother.

'A person walking on the spiritual path at some point will find their natural inclination to worship their Kul Devi or Devta. It'll happen effortlessly,' He said.

Much to my surprise, a fortnight or so after my initiation, I had a dream of the Lord's *Viraat Swaroopa*. I was sleeping in my pooja room when I had this dream. A picture of Sri Hari and Swamiji was on my altar and a lamp burnt by its side.

In the dream, I was surrounded by pristine whiteness. There were no clouds or blue sky, everything was whiter than anything I had ever seen. Tall pillars stood in a semi-circle as in an amphitheater, with marble stairs leading to some place I could not see. In that milky whiteness, a bright silken dhoti, *pitamabara,* the colour of burnt mustard flapped in the air. I felt Bhagavān's feet, rather than seeing them, I felt their presence. As my eyes moved up, His long legs wrapped in the brilliant shining *pitamabra* stood tall. The further up my eyes moved, the taller Bhagavān seemed to be, frantically my eyes searched for a face, but His thighs seemed never-ending. There was no end to Him, not even a hint of a waist.

When my eyes had travelled far and beyond, with neither the sky nor clouds in sight, only His long limbs, in my dream I had a realization that Bhagavān wasn't revealing Himself to me. I woke up with a start, thinking that maybe Bhagavān didn't show me His face because it's Swamiji's face. And He doesn't want me to know that just yet. The whiteness of that realm, those gigantic white pillars no humans could have made and loftier than those pillars were Bhagavān's unending legs. I don't know what I had seen, but I knew *who* I had seen. His presence had been undeniable. Still, the human mind is so enmeshed in the world that Bhagavān would walk by and it'd remain clueless and ignorant. Much later, I heard Swamiji say in a discourse in the temple that when one is initiated into a lineage, the deity of that lineage shows up to give their blessings in a dream.

I never shared this with anyone, not even Swamiji, thinking that He'll think me silly. And that He'd most certainly deny it.

Any reference to Him as Bhagavān or a powerful entity is laughed away and almost always He'd say, 'If I was Bhagavān don't you think I'd have fixed this or that.'

It's amusing to Him and He'll have you believe that you are being daft thinking such things. He's a simple sadhu with some siddhis, is the furthest He may allow your imagination to wander. But the things I'd go on to witness in His presence said otherwise.

The Divine Greeting

Bhakti tat anupam sukhmula, milen hi jo sant hoi anukula, devotion is the basis of unparalleled bliss, but you only experience devotion with the grace of a saint or guru... I had heard Swamiji say this couplet from Ramcharitmanas on more than one occasion. It had been absolutely true for me and naturally, I was delighted beyond words when I came across the *chaupai*, couplet, while reading the scripture.

I didn't think that a simple reading would bring such a shift in my perspective or make my heart mushy with devotion for Bhagavān but I knew one thing: it was my Guru's instruction. And so, I followed it like a calf follows its mother.

It took two months to read the Ramcharitmanas. In the end, Lord Rama's victory felt like a triumph over my own *vikaras*, vices. My outlook underwent a great change towards Bhagavān. He was indeed Purushottama, the finest among men. Swamiji had been clear from the start that I needed to understand the verses rather than chant them out loud. While I was reading the Bal-Kand which covered Prince Rama's childhood and exile, I felt quite moved by His love and regard for the three Queen mothers.

There wasn't a moment's delay to obey Queen Kekeyi and King Dashrath when Bhagavān was asked to live in exile for fourteen years. It moved me deeply, for never in my life could I've imagined acting so selflessly. And to my great sorrow, the one person in the Ramayana, thus far, I felt whose personality matched mine was Queen Kekeyi. I had always been so selfish that she and I seemed like we were cut from the same cloth. It obviously saddened me deeply.

I confessed to Swamiji about the affinity I felt with the unkind Queen. He was quite amused at my pick of her.

'Come now, yes, you can be difficult at times but that doesn't make you Kekeyi. You are unnecessarily identifying with her.'

'Thank you, Swamiji, it's such a relief to hear that from you.'

Chuckling He said, 'Though you can be a bit melodramatic, Sadhviji.'

By the time I finished the beautiful scripture, I found the perfect character whom I wished to be like. It wasn't Lord Hanuman, Maa Sita or Shabri or a host of other wonderfully devoted people, how could I ever hope to possess devotion like them?

Since more than anything else in the world, I wished to have the wisdom and discernment to know Bhagavān and myself. It was Bharat, Lord Rama's younger brother, in the end whom I felt a great affinity with. He had great wisdom and devotion for his Lord Rama and waited for Him fourteen years to return from exile. From Kekeyi to Bharat was my little journey, and as Swamiji had predicted, it instilled a sense of deep reverence in my heart. There's a *chaupai* in Ramcharitmanas that says that taking the Lord's name can purge you of your sins.

दुर्लभ मानुष देह पावा । हरि लेन दुर्भाग्य नष जावा ॥
तुलसी तात सम मोहि भाई । जगदम्ब सम हि रुप न तातई ॥

'Obtaining a human body is rare, but through taking the name of Hari unfortunate souls are purified. O brother! Tulsi says that there is no one like Jagadamba (the Divine Mother) in all the three worlds.'

From then on, I decided that I'd greet everyone by taking Bhagavān's name. It'd keep myself mentally calm and purify my speech and heart. I started with saying *Jai Sri Krishna*, as I had heard Matarani and some others say. But it felt too long and didn't roll as easily off my tongue. *Jai Sri Ram* was next, and I stuck to it for a little while, until, I greeted Swamiji one day like that.

'But we have Sri Hari here, so, won't Jai Sri Ram feel a bit odd to anyone who visits the ashram?' He said quite amused with the new thing I had started. 'Of course, there's no difference whatsoever but the visitors to the ashram will be searching for Dhanurdhari Rama in our idol.'

'You are right, Swamiji, I'll think of something else.'

I tried a few more permutations and combinations and came up with *Jai Sri Hari*. There was no looking back from there, no matter what greeting was offered to me, my response was always the same *Jai Sri Hari*. It caught on soon enough in the ashram and went on to become the standard greeting in the years to come.

It was wonderfully funny how both Vidya Swami and Swamiji imitated the way I said *Jai Sri Hari* in the initial days. There was just always so much affection and warmth in Swamiji's presence that life couldn't be more beautiful. Such innocence, in His manner of speaking, looking at the world, at you, that every day in His service my heart melted. And it wasn't just happening to me, it happened to everyone, disciples, devotees, strangers who came to see Him from far. Like the sun doesn't discriminate upon whom the sunlight falls, so it was with Swamiji; whoever was in His orbit felt the force of His goodness and divinity.

Guru Mantra

My first sadhana was of the powerful Guru mantra I had been blessed with by my Guru. To thank Him, for His grace was my foremost desire. It was during the sadhana I realized that initiation had sprung a bridge of sorts, where, in my mind's eye, if I focused right, I could sense Swamiji's presence. I could see His face with a clarity that astounded me. It wasn't a constant thing. It was more like a light fluctuation that came and went. It has only deepened over the years, with a slight change though. As I see Swamiji more and more as Sri Hari, the face that appears in my japa is also Sri Hari's.

In my mantra japa, focusing on its sound was the original intention but the mind, time and again, would find its way to Swamiji's undeniably beautiful and divine face. Having no prior experience with mantras or any serious meditation, I'd just flow with wherever the mind carried me, and no matter how many detours it made, it'd always end up thinking of Him. So, when His face came into focus, at first, I wasn't surprised.

He was, is, and always has been the object of my *dhyana*, and finding Him inside my head is as natural as finding fish in water. So, what was different about Swamiji's presence in my head that morning? It was a manifestation and not an image of Him from my memory. My mind hadn't conjured Him, the vision had come to me, just as Sri Hari had appeared in my head calling me for His aarti.

On this day, I felt in my Agya chakra, the brow plexus, a beautiful light. It was like being close to the sun. My mind was suddenly a thought-less clearing where the smiling sun of Swamiji's face shone in my face. It was a big face, round and fair, sharp and full of laughter, made more luminous by a garland of white and pale-yellow flowers around His neck. A *yajnopavita*, the sacred thread, went around His chest. He wore a cotton dhoti, the colour of dark turmeric. Oh God, it suited Him so much.

On His beaming forehead shone two *tilakams*, one was vermillion and the other was a dark yellow tilak. Strangely, it was this *tilakam* that caught my attention. I had never seen a *tilak* like that one before. His health, too, seemed much better than in real life. He seemed to glow as a candle illumines a dark wall. His head shining like a *tapasvi's*, a holy sage. He was not the Swamiji I met every day. He wasn't of my world. And it wasn't just the garland on His chest or the bright yellow dhoti, it was just the way He was, different, *Godlike*.

In rapt attention, I held on to this smiling manifestation that seemed ancient, like a page out of an olden time. The more intensely and intently I looked at Him, the more He smiled. For as long as my feeble mind could hold on to Him, I did, smiling at His beautiful vision before it exploded into a ball of light, leaving an empty space in my head.

As soon as my japa got over, I ran to offer my pranams to Swamiji, who had just finished His breakfast. The morning sunlight streamed through the glass windows of His study, making everything around Him bright and beautiful. I was tongue-tied at first, for I had just seen Him a little while back but now He seemed different.

'Swamiji, you had a garland, you were wearing a yellow dhoti and a *yajnopavita*. Do I sound crazy?'

Swamiji seemed so relaxed after His breakfast, quiet like the sky and there I was rambling and rattling like a snake.

'And there was a strange tilak, Swamiji, what was that...'

'Gopi Kesar Chandan,' He answered, before I could finish.

Swamiji!' I shrieked, 'Please tell me what I just saw.'

A mysterious and mischievous smile played on His lips as He simply uttered two words, 'The Vamana Avatar.'

All the curiosity, the questions, like a fire doused by water fell flat just like that. For it made perfect sense, I had seen Him in that *Swaroopa*, form, with my own eyes. The revelation stumped me, and I didn't know what more to ask or how. How do you ask your Guru, what did it mean that He had just given me a vision of the Vamana Avtara, the fifth incarnation of Lord Vishnu? Was it Him or something else entirely? I neither had the courage to ask, nor the intelligence to frame a question after such an admission. I just knew that what I had seen was the reality. I had seen it in a fully conscious state at 8 am in the morning.

S - Srivatsa

In the city, my neighbors, Deepa and Bhupen, a loving couple provided great support to my black Lab, Benoo and me. When Deepa saw me for the first time, as I walked Benoo on a crowded street, she had said to her daughter, Ashu, 'This young girl lives all by herself...there's some divine power protecting her.'

It had become a routine that one meal I ate at Deepa's place. After my sannyasa, Matarani had sent a beautiful silver thali, plate, along with silverware and bowls, as it's considered auspicious to serve sannyasis in the same. Deepa began serving me food in it. After I donned the ochre robe, Bhupen and Deepa's care turned to a deep regard. It had everything to do with the fact that none other than Om Swami was my Guru. They had experienced a great dramatic shift in their emotional and financial state with Swamiji's advent in their life. And I became the recipient of all their love and gratitude towards Him.

Deepa managed the indoor stuff for me in the city with care and fondness, and all the outdoor odd jobs, Bhupen took over.

On the eve of Krishna Janmashtami, which fell on 25th August 2016, nearly a month after my *deeksha*, something incredible happened. It was 8 pm and I had just finished a sumptuous dinner at Deepa's house. I knelt before their altar, where a beautiful picture of Swamiji, an 8-inch by 8-inch photo frame was kept.

It was a habit that each time I came to their house or was leaving, I'd bow to Swamiji's photo. I did the same that night, said my goodbyes to the kids and had reached the main door, when I felt like something was calling me. I turned back and without thinking walked all the way back to the altar and for no comprehensible reason peered closely at Swamiji's picture.

To my astonishment and annoyance someone had drawn a 'S' shape with a pen on Swamiji's chest. I quickly called Deepa, who was in the kitchen clearing up.

'What's this mark, who made this?'

'What do you mean, Sadhviji?' Deepa asked. Sensing a note of distress in my tone, everyone crowded around the picture. The three kids and husband-wife were equally surprised, they hadn't seen it before. I thought maybe one of their teenage children had done so. But everyone was as surprised as me. We marveled at the shining mark on the photo. It was as if someone had drawn a S, with a silver glitter pen.

'It wasn't there this morning,' Bhupen said as he routinely did his Ramayana recitation in front of the altar every morning.

'It wasn't there at lunch time, too,' I piped in, as I always touched my hand to Swamiji's picture and hadn't noticed anything out of the ordinary when I had come for lunch.

Suddenly, it occurred to me that maybe the mark had appeared just now. Could it be why Bhagavān had summoned me back from the main-door and straight to the photo? We were all so shocked and tried to make some sense out of it.

Ashu went and got a wet cloth and we gently tried to wipe it, but we couldn't. It was as if printed, etched upon, Swamiji's photo. It remained intact, even when we tried to gently scratch it. There was nothing to scrape, it was a part of the photo.

There was also a warm halo upon Swamiji's head and chest. But that could have been attributed to anything, maybe the picture paper was fading, although, how it could have faded in one day is anybody's guess. But the mark, we just couldn't explain it away, Nothing could. It was so clear, so visible, so solid, there was no explanation whatsoever. A capital S, silvery and sparkly just stared back at us.

In the later days, when we tried to make copies of the photo with the mark, we couldn't. The mark doesn't show up on a photo negative of the original or when copied in a photocopier. The only way to make copies was to click a picture of the original photo, and then get duplicates made.

After we were tired of making sense of the mark, I ran up to my house and emailed Swamiji. In all this commotion half an hour had passed. With trembling hands I wrote about the bizarre mark to Him.

I eagerly waited to hear from Him. His email, when it came the next day, simply blew my mind away.

It's the mark of Srivatsa that has appeared on the photo.

In the second half of the 64th verse of Vishnu Sahasranama, it says:

श्रीवत्सवक्षाः श्रीवासः श्रीपतिः श्रीमतांवरः ॥ 64 ॥

śrīvatsavakṣāḥ śrīvāsaḥ śrīpatiḥ śrīmatāṃvaraḥ || *64*

Lord Vishnu carries the mark of Srivatsa right on His chest.

Mother Divine has appeared to bless the family because they look after you, care for you with love, Sadhviji. Maa Annapurna has blessed them. There'll never be any shortage of food or any lack in their home.

It touches me deeply that you aren't alone there, and that family is there to look after you. For this reason, they'll always have my protection.

The next day, I told Deepa and the family about the mark and Swamiji's blessing but adjusted the part about my involvement. I felt both shy and undeserving of such grace at Swamiji's hands. His magnanimity was limitless and without any cause or demand. He just gave and gave and gave until, one had no choice but to raise their hands in surrender. It's been six years now and the mark remains intact, just as bright and vivid as when it first appeared on the eve of Krishna Janmasthmi.

My life since Swamiji's arrival has only been filled with miracles after miracles. I had often wondered why such grace on me. I had no special qualities, rather a restless mind that could destroy everything good in a matter of moments. It wasn't like I was bringing some great joy to Swamiji. For the better part, I was always drowning in doom and gloom, combative and ever whining about how I didn't want to live. Then why Swamiji protected me at every step, was something I could never understand back then.

How powerful was He that the Divine Mother came at His behest to shower blessings on a nobody like me? It was a mystery the answer to which I stopped looking for after a while, believing that maybe I was special, after all, for such amazing things to happen to me. He even had a cute name for me, just like Swami Vidyananda was Motu, Swamiji nicknamed me, Bhikkuram, derived from Bhikku or disciple, in the Pali language. So, why wouldn't I have airs that there was something different about me. As they say every frog in a pond thinks that he's a prince and every pumpkin in the field is eager to be Cinderella's ride. I was happy being an ignorant frog and a pumpkin with aspirations.

Vaikuntha

As I sit down to recall this particular incident on a summer day of April 2023, Swamiji has already left for five months of solitude and the ashram has less than twenty residents. I'm sitting by the temple steps, gazing at Sri Hari's beautiful face. My darling Mother is resplendent in a khadi-silk, purple sari, a colour my mamma loved very much when she was alive. I believe it to be a sign from Mother Divine for the task at hand I have today.

Earlier in the day, there was another sign. On the way to my room from the temple, I saw a baby bird on the ground. She appeared like a napping puppy, her beak tilted to one side, a hair-less body, and a tiny sack for a tummy. Her deformed wings and webbed claws were a sorry sight as she lay dead amidst a bunch of fallen straw from the roof. I winced involuntarily, mentally offering her safe passage to Sri Hari. My immediate next thought was how heartbroken the mother-bird would be on finding her baby lying like that. It made me want to cry. I felt pained at the thought and quickly blinked back tears for her poor mother.

When I was in my early 30s, living at home, I never understood why mamma agonized so much over what was going to happen to me. Life was, for better or worse, a certain way for both her and me. We were alone, miserable, and waiting for something beautiful to happen to us. That maybe one day, something big would transpire and life would pick up pace. She died waiting for that to happen, and in the end, all she wanted was for me to have a life different than hers had been. I knew mamma loved me, but selfishly, I had no idea how deep a mother's love for her daughter is, until Swamiji showed up.

Seeing the dead baby-bird made me think of her mother and in turn of mine. It is no coincidence that I was due to write this particular chapter today. Already since morning, Garuda Bhagwan has circled above my head right outside the temple, as if signaling his blessings, as I divulge the Parabrahma aspect of Swamiji.

It's also incidentally, the day when the dutiful, devoted and seva-loving Prabhu Swami offered aarti to Sri Hari for the very first time since his sannyasa. With so much happening before 8 am, my mind was filled with great love for the Divine and their boundless munificence.

So, let me now rewind the clock to 8th September 2016, mamma's death anniversary. It had been four years since her passing, and I didn't feel as terrible a daughter for not doing more for her. The pain was almost gone, just that when I felt really lonely or something nice happened to me, I missed her.

On the morning of mamma's death anniversary, I especially sought Swamiji's blessings in person. I requested Him to give mamma my love, wherever she was. It was just like any other day in His tranquil presence, a beautiful one. His hands, long and fair rested by His side. He is so beautiful that it always takes me, or anyone for that matter, a few minutes to fully adjust to His holy presence. It's always the same for me.

Everything felt quieter that day. He wasn't His usual busy self, pressed for time, meetings, which in itself was a strange phenomenon. I stayed seated a little longer than usual. Vidya Swami had just stepped out to get Swamiji's coffee.

I was sitting by Swamiji's feet when He said,

'I'm going to chant something now, Bhikkuram, just listen,' Adjusting His robe to one side, placing His hand on my head, He sang a hymn. He sang softly at first but soon His voice turned into a deep base. I didn't understand the long, lyrical Sanskrit verses but their hypnotic power was undeniable.

I had closed my eyes a while back and my ears focused on His voice. In the time that my mind started to relax into the hymn, the face of my dead mother, beautiful, radiant and alive appeared out of nowhere. One moment, my mind was filled with the usual thoughts and the next, everything had been swept aside by force, for her to take center stage. She was just there. Her young face, of no more than 26 years, loomed large in my mind's eye.

Her lovely Kashmiri features and the diamond nose-pin she always wore cast a dazzling shine upon my mind. Her eyes sparkled with love, as she looked straight at me. I was so startled, I cried, 'mamma'. Tears rolled down my eyes and mamma's eyes started watering too. But she seemed to be crying out of happiness to see me. *What was happening? It couldn't be real; this vision would vanish any moment.*

The chant became quicker, but Swamiji was still like a mountain.

It was as if with His will alone He was holding my mother there, in my head.

I didn't dare open my eyes for the fear that I might not see her again. This was my dead mother, whom I hadn't seen in four years. And the last I had seen of her was on an ICU bed, with a hole in her jugular, her body weighing nearly 81 kgs due to kidney failure. Her face white as chalk and eyes sad beyond words. Here she was so alive, healthy and young like an *apsara*, nymph, in heaven. Between confusion and elation on seeing her, I felt a twinge of envy spring in my consciousness on how attractive she had become. That feeling had lasted no longer than a second. In all that time, I never stopped crying, I couldn't. I tried to say to her that I wished I had been a better daughter to her. But her loving face, the joy and pride in her eyes, squashed every other thought away.

To see mamma joyous and well, healed something inside of me. I almost reached out with my arm to touch her. Slowly, as a baby is separated from a mother's arms, her vision started to fade. The brilliance surrounding her face began receding.

I tried to hold on to her, but she was gone, and I realized Swamiji had fallen silent too. I opened my tear-filled eyes to find Him looking at me with great compassion.

'Mamma was very happy to see you, Bhikkuram,' He said in the gentlest voice. I wept like a child on hearing Him say that.

'How's it possible, Swamiji, she's alive?' I said struggling to string the words together, 'Where is she?'

'She's safe in Vaikuntha.'

I was still reeling from the shock of seeing her to grasp the actual import of these words.

'Mamma's with you. She looks so…' I said.

'Did you feel a bit envious?' He intervened and chuckled. 'Oh my God, you know that too,' I said embarrassed. As if I wasn't freaked enough already, He had caught every vague, fleeting thought and feeling in my head, even as He had chanted the hymn.

'How is she so beautiful and so happy, Swamiji?'

'No one ever ages in Vaikuntha, there's no illness or grief.'

Who was He really? By then, I was as good as gasping for air.

'I know you miss her very much. I just wanted you to see that she's well and very happy and proud to see you in ochre, as am I.'

It was all too much to make sense of. As the tears flowed unabated, I thanked Him profusely for giving me a place by His feet. From somewhere a line from Swamiji's discourse evening came to me:

'And when somebody loses their parents, one who loses their mother or father, they can never return to this world no matter how much you pray or want them to come back.'

Then how had Swamiji brought alive a vision of my mother? He had also transported her to the most coveted place mentioned in the Vedic scriptures - Vaikuntha. Had someone told me of such an incident I'd never have believed them no matter how credible they appeared to be. It was only possible in a story. But I had seen her myself. How do I un-see that?

Imagine that you wake up screaming at night and your family gathers around you wanting to know what has happened. You say to them as coherently as is possible in such a situation that you've seen a thief in the house. They start searching the house, checking the doors and windows. Everything is locked and sealed tight. There isn't a trace of him. No one believes you because there's no way the thief could have entered the house. But you saw him. Even if for the briefest of time, you were face to face with the thief. You stand your ground, and everyone starts to think you are paranoid. Are you paranoid?

For you alone know what your eyes have seen, and the heart has felt, there's no going back from it. Mamma had looked every bit lovely, well and thriving in this eternal place, and just like a thief she was gone, as quietly as she had come, robbing me of her affections, once again.

sarva-bhūteṣhu yenaikaṁ bhāvam avyayam īkṣhate
avibhaktaṁ vibhakteṣhu taj jñānaṁ viddhi sāttvikam.

The one established in a *sattvic bhava*, mode of goodness, sees one undivided, imperishable reality within all diverse sentient beings.

Bhagavad Gita, 18.20.

The Other Life

Sniffling like an old lady, I tried hard not to cry. But I just couldn't stop. Swamiji passed me the tissue box. Vidya Swami had strict instructions to keep the tissue box near at all times, as most people broke down in Swamiji's presence, either in pain or joy or in gratefulness. It was customary and a frequent occurrence, it's why Swamiji preferred the tissue box be handy. In the past I had found it funny that He would ensure that the tissue box was close by at all times. Today, it wasn't funny, it was a life saver. After I was done crying, I asked Him something that occurred to me.

'What would have happened to me had you not found me, Swamiji?'

'Why discuss things that haven't happened? It's pointless.' Seeing Him gently evade my question only made me plead more persistently.

Relenting, He said, 'Your brother, Sunny would have gone abroad to work. You'd have stayed with Benoo in Pune, all alone for the next three years, and by the end of 2016 you'd have met someone and settled with him.'

'Would I have been happy with him?'

'Well, not as happy as you are here. All worldly relationships come with their fair share of stress... and no, you wouldn't have had any children if that's what you are thinking.'

Oh God, it's exactly what I was thinking because I never really wanted children. *Can one hide anything from Him at all?*

'What about afterwards?'

He was quiet for a moment and said, 'You might have had to have chemo...'

'Chemo as in chemotherapy?' I said wide-eyed and surprised. These are things that happen to other people, you never imagine it happening to you.

Seeing my terrified expression, He laughed and said, 'Oh, nothing would have happened to you, as I keep saying you've a long life like your Grandpa,' He paused to chuckle, 'But there'd have been routine trips to the hospital all your life.'

This conversation ended here as He refused to answer more questions about a future that no longer existed. The course of my future changed irreversibly when His saintly feet had walked into my life.

It was impossible, henceforth, for me to not view Him in a different light. He was no longer human to me. He had his own realm, where people looked like movie stars and were always happy. I wasn't yet wise or even mature enough to know what I had witnessed, but I knew it was as real as you see another person sitting next to you.

Truth be told, after this incident, I was also a little afraid of Swamiji. He wasn't just my Guru. He was like God Himself, moving about in the world, championing strays and underdogs like me. He was so powerful, He could do anything, and yet, He is the kindest person I have ever met.

In Eknath Easwaran's book, *Vishnu and His Thousand Names*, he explains Bhagavān's name – *Bhutabhavana*, Essence of All Beings. This particular name might explain how Swamiji by the power of His thought had brought me face to face with my late mother.

Here's the excerpt:

> *It is worth a few moments of reflection to grasp what it means to say that God has become all things. In an age that tinkers with genes and speculates about the first three minutes of creation, we may forget to wonder about the world we live in and how little of it even our sciences can grasp. We know, for example, that light travels at about 186,000 miles per second. We know that fact, yet it is quite another thing to understand it.*
>
> *Imagine, as young Einstein did, that you had a long ray of light like a commuter train, and that you could sit astride this ray as you sit on the five-fifteen express and travel at the speed of light. It would take only a second and a quarter to reach the moon; one blink of an eye and you would be there. In eight minutes—the time it takes to get to the nearest supermarket—you would reach the sun. Yet you would have to sit there on that magical ray for four years to reach the nearest star, and you could travel that way for one hundred thousand years and never get out of our same old Milky Way. Imagine the expanse!*
>
> *Then for two million more years it is just empty space—no gas stations, no Holiday Inns—until you reach the nearest neighboring galaxy. There are believed to be two hundred*

billion galaxies within the observable universe, each of them containing perhaps a hundred billion suns. It's not even the whole picture, yet we still can't grasp it; we can't absorb what these figures mean.

Suppose one science writer suggests, that you are willing to work eight hours a day, seven days a week—no days off to tend to the yard—counting at the rate of one number every second. It will take a month to reach one million, a relatively small figure on our scale. If you want to understand one billion, this writer says, keep counting in the same way—no coffee breaks, no vacations, no union slowdowns—until the end of your life. I said to myself, 'Yes, sir, I get the point.'

Most intriguing, perhaps, is why astronomers are so careful to say, 'the observable universe.' It doesn't mean only 'That's all we can see for now,' as if some day, with more powerful telescopes in orbit beyond the moon, we might be able to see it all. If Einstein was right, as a good deal of careful observation still bears out, then we can never 'see' the whole universe.

The speed of light itself limits us to a kind of bubble of observation in space-time, beyond which we simply cannot perceive. No messages can reach us from beyond that bubble, and none can be sent. But that does not mean there is nothing beyond; these are merely restrictions on the delivery service. Worse yet, as soon as we start looking any significant distance into this bubble, we find we are seeing things not as they are but as they were.

Wherever we look in the starry sky, we are looking quite literally at the past. One star appears to lie next to another, but actually we see each of them as it was when that light set out on its journey. One of those stars might have been destroyed centuries ago in the explosion of a supernova; we cannot know. We devote special attention to a star, analyze its spectrum to see what it is made of, guess at its past and future evolution, and while we are guessing, that 'future' has happened, and the star may be gone! If it is a thousand light years away, the news of its death would not reach us for a thousand years.

The Crab nebula represents the remains of a supernova explosion observed by Chinese astronomers in A.D. 1054, but the actual explosion took place about 3000 B.C. Even the constellations whose names have come to us down the ages may suffer from severe generation gaps: the stars in them may be separated by thousands of years, as we measure from here on earth.

Space and time, bound together, inevitably limit and distort the validity of what we can say about the universe. But these dimensions do not apply to the Lord. In the Hindu scriptures we find the provoking statement that this vast cosmos is one thought of the Lord. That is as long as our universe lasts: one thought.

Avibhaktam vibhakteshu, Swamiji often quotes from the Bhagavad Gita saying that for the one firmly established in the mode of goodness, there are no separate individual embodied souls but simply one supreme soul. For such a person the boundaries of time and space disappear. That is precisely how I have seen Him operate on countless occasions.

A Cure

In December 2015, we travelled to Bangalore for the launch of Swamiji's incredible book on meditation, *A Million Thoughts*. Thereafter, a four-day Zen meditation retreat had been organized at the outskirts of Bangalore at the Golden Palms resort.

True to its name, it had tall palm trees, beautiful blooming frangipanis and lush greenery surrounding the cottages. It was a lovely place and even lovelier were Swamiji's sessions on the art of meditation. During one of the sessions, Swamiji had made us walk mindfully by forming a line, where each person rested their one arm on the shoulder of the person in front. This walking Zen meditation was called Kinhin. Except for the person in front, everyone's eyes were closed, and like the boxes of a train follow the engine, we had moved about trusting the person in front. I was one of the people to lead a train of people around. It was a beautiful and fun exercise.

On the second morning of our stay, a small group of people, namely the graceful Matarani, Didi (Swamiji's radiant sister), Sanjeev Madan, a few more devotees, Vidya Swami and myself, sat with Swamiji in His open suite facing a beautiful row of palms.

A soft breeze was blowing in and Swamiji seemed relaxed as the event was soon coming to a close. He was telling us how the carpet in His bedroom had so much dust that it seemed it had never been dry-cleaned. It was so delightful to see His pink cheeks turn pinker as He laughed, making us all feel like little children in the presence of their most favorite grandparent.

A little while later, Matarani softly said to Swamiji that Didi had a persistent headache the whole night and had been quite unwell since her arrival.

'She will not say, Swamiji, so I had to,' Matarani said looking up at Swamiji's face, with anxious eyes. Post Didi's brain surgery many years ago, her health could be a bit fragile at times.

Swamiji was immediately concerned, and He asked Didi to come and sit closer to Him, so He could place His hand on her head. As a father places his hand on a child's head and gently kneads it, Swamiji's hand moved on His sister's head. Even though, Didi is older to Swamiji by six years, the equation between them is quite reverse. She always treats Him with great reverence and respect, as if He's the elder one. In a matter of seconds her tired face began to relax, and a soft smile appeared on her face. A minute later, Didi's headache had all but disappeared.

'It's gone,' she said folding her hands and thanking Him.

Swamiji smiled at her, 'You are welcome, Didi.'

And then He looked straight at me and raised an eyebrow, and I couldn't help laughing as I said, 'Thank you, Swamiji, I'm all good too, now.'

Everyone looked at me and a little shyly I explained to everyone that I had a splitting headache too. But I obviously hadn't said anything. When Swamiji had placed His hand on Didi's head, it was as if He was kneading my head too. As if I was the primary recipient of the energy transfer. The weight of His hand upon my head was unmistakable, when it was actually Didi on whose head His hand rested. I don't know how that was even possible.

I was sitting at least a few meters away. And I hadn't even said anything about my headache, He just knew. In a couple of minutes, He had cured both Didi and me. Mind blowing as it was, nothing in His presence surprised me anymore.

Six months into sannyasa and I was beginning to see the true face of my Guru. He wasn't just allaying the fears of others but mine too. Fears in my own ability to let Him down. I no longer laughed or scoffed at myself internally when Swamiji asked me to take up things I had never done before. So, when He asked me to spread Bhagavān's glories by doing *kirtan* and satsangs in the homes of devotees, I dived right in.

I knew He was powering me. Anyone who asked for His grace with deep devotion in their heart would find it, without even having ever seen Him. I just had to be there, to let people know that He was here, amidst us and people at the right time would receive his grace.

For the universe is not bound by any religion or rituals, but by the depth and purity of one's connection to that Divine power that has as many names as the number of people on this planet. And when Swamiji said, 'You must sing Bhagavān's glories, Sadhviji. It's what you are destined to do.'

I could only marvel at such a destiny. I longed for nothing more than singing His glories, whether it be *kirtan*, satsangs or books. He had given me so much, beyond my worthiness. I wasn't waiting for people to wake up to the power of satsang, I had to wake them up right now.

ananyacetāḥ satataṁ yo māṁ smarati nityaśaḥ |
tasyāhaṁ sulabhaḥ pārtha nityayuktasya yoginaḥ ||14||

O' Partha! I am easily attainable to the ever-steadfast Yogi, who constantly remembers Me at all times with undivided attention.

Bhagavad Gita, 8.14.

2017

Summons

Some of the most beautiful memories with Swamiji for most old-timers are of the old meeting room where Swamiji sat on an old-style village cot giving discourses and meeting people. I don't remember the exact month, but it was winter. I was doing my morning japa in the temple and in a brilliant halo in my mind's eye Swamiji's gently smiling face appeared. It stayed a while and since, I was a newbie, I could barely muster an image of my choosing, my object of worship, let alone hold it for more than two seconds, I knew this wasn't my doing. Swamiji's face shining inside my head like the warm winter Sun was there for a reason. It was a summon.

Wrapping up my japa in the next five minutes, I ran to the old meeting room. Outside, there were many people waiting for their turn to meet their Guru. Swami Parmananda (the PA back then; Swamiji likes to keep this role in rotation depending on the need of that time) was managing Swamiji's meeting schedule. I had waited only a minute when Swamiji's PA opened the door. I said, 'Swamiji was calling me.'

Stepping in, I started speaking right away, 'Swamiji, did you just call me.'

'Aava, baitha, come sit.' Smiling gently, He pointed to the mat in a playful Bhojpuri accent.

Raghu Swamiji was already sitting there, moving his arms left and right in his childlike manner as he observed his beloved Guru.

I looked up to find to Swamiji's left was the most beautiful Panch Dhatu Bhagavān of Sri Hari. If my memory serves me right, it was two and a half feet tall or a little less. The colour of matt gold and resplendent like our Sri Hari in the temple. I asked Swamiji about it.

'Will tell you in a moment,' He said, looking at the door. Just then the meeting room door opened, and Vidya Swami walked in, surprised to see all the sannyasis there. The one person who wasn't surprised was Swamiji.

I thought to myself, Vidya Swami never comes at this time to see Swamiji. What's really going on?

Vidya Swami said he wasn't sure why he had come; he had simply taken a detour. He was apologetic, thinking he had barged in an important meeting. Swamiji beckoned him as well, to sit. Now all four of us were looking at Swamiji to tell us why we were here. Swamiji gazed at the Bhagavān next to Him, admiring Bhagavān's expression and weapons. He said, 'A long-time devotee from Canada, Sunil ji, has brought this Bhagavān for consecration. And see how Bhagavān has summoned all of you from different corners of the ashram at the same time.'

'But why Swamiji?' I asked perplexed.

'All four of you were there in 2014 when we first opened the box in which Sri Hari had arrived. You were there when Bhagavān was made to stand in the temple. Sri Hari wanted all of you to be here, just like that day.'

I looked around the room and it was the exact same arrangement from the day we had unwrapped Sri Hari on 16th March 2014, the eve of Holi. It had happened fifteen days before the consecration ceremony! There was Bhagavān standing majestically, Swamiji right next to Him, Vidya Swami, Raghu Swami, Parmananda Swami and me.

The only difference was that I was a Sannyasi now. Back then there had been other village folk and people as well, but Swamiji had only asked me to step inside (the under construction *garbhagriha*) to assist in unwrapping Sri Hari from the bubble wrap and packing. And while everyone was busy taking off the bubble wrap, I had quickly torn the wrapping from Bhagavān's face, so eager was I to see Him. I had gently caressed His cheeks in awe. He was different then, straight out of the box and yet, the eyes had twinkled just like they do today. I felt very much like a child then as much as I do in His grandiose presence today. A slight shift in the equation since then is that some days He appears like a child to me...my child.

In the years that have followed since, all has unfolded like a grand design. Perhaps that's why they say that all that a *bhakta* needs, the Lord provides unfailingly.

Finding Euro

This is a dog-story, unlike any you've ever read or heard. Love is such a beautiful thing that it keeps pulling you into its fold like a soft warm quilt in winter. No matter where you are, the thought of the one you love, keeps running parallel to everything that's going on in your life, in your mind. You want to see them, be with them. Their quirks, laughter, and joys are the things that actually keep you afloat. You are tied to them by a very strong and tangible thread. In my case, Benoo was that beautiful black thread with a lovely shiny coat and the most adorable greedy-green-eyes. I'd frequently return to the city, a mere three hours' drive from the ashram to spend time with her.

On one such visit, I was just stepping off the lift to have my lunch at Deepa's, when I saw a tall young lady in her late twenties sobbing in the corridor. Some other people were also there along with Deepa trying to calm her down. She was inconsolable, wailing like a child. I thought maybe someone had died or had a major accident. I quickly asked Deepa what's going on and how I could help.

It seemed the someone had stolen the lady's eleven-month old-beagle. She had taken him for a walk and when she looked around, he wasn't there. She was besides herself with grief. I understood her pain. The thought of losing Benoo was something that could push me to the edge, so the lady's reaction didn't seem out of place to me at all.

Since morning, many search parties had gone searching the society premises, but no one heard or saw anything. The guards at the gate didn't see anyone take a dog outside. The only theory was that maybe he had been smuggled in a car. The entire building was gathered there, as the wails of the young woman were hard to ignore for anyone, dog-lover or not. It's like her child had been abducted. Please believe me when I say the scenario completely shook me - what if it was Benoo.

I quickly ran up to email Swamiji. No problem was too big or small for Him. He would know what to do, I thought. You might think why would I call upon Him for every small thing, but there actually was no one in my life to turn to. And more than anything else, He never disappointed me; whether the matter was big or small, of life or death, He always resolved it for me.

Also, there was a good reason behind my wanting to ask for His help. I was afraid to handle this by myself. In 2015, when I once took Benoo for a stroll outside on the main road, a confrontation with some local people had transpired. One of them had called a lady constable in civilian clothes, who lived close by and forcibly tried to take Benoo's leash from my hands. She figured that was my Achilles' heel. She then slapped me hard across the face and pushed me while trying to set Benoo loose. Swamiji was very upset when He had heard the news and since then asked me to be extremely careful in the city.

'Sometimes people are so vicious, but no one is above the law of karma,' he said.

And so, in a very disturbed state of mind, I emailed Swamiji to find Euro, the beagle.

When His email came, He only sent a one-liner:

His chances of coming back are dim, now how important is it to you that we find Euro?

In my response, I implored, begged Him to find Euro.

Everyone had given up hope, all avenues were exhausted, it seemed like a lost cause. The next morning, lo and behold, Euro was returned, left outside the lady's door. I was so elated and couldn't stop thanking Swamiji enough. I knew Swamiji would find him. The lady in question organized a *jagaran,* as she had pledged that if Euro came home, she would feed everyone and there would be Maa's *langar.*

She also came home to thank me as Deepa apprised her that I made it happen. Which wasn't true but everyone was just happy that they got to take Devi Maa's name and had sumptuous *langar* food. As for Euro, he was washed, bathed and pampered like never before. He returned home a star and children and women lined outside to see him. It was a funny scene but because we had been so closely involved, it only brought us relief.

That night, I had a nightmare. I saw Swamiji sitting in a chair, haggard and unwell. He was in a black robe, His face chalk like and He could barely sit. He seemed extremely unwell and an IV ran up His forearm. He was so weak that when He tried to get up, He just fell back in the chair. On seeing Him so vulnerable and fragile, I wailed loudly.

I experienced so much pain at seeing Him defenseless, for I have only ever seen Him strong like a rock. In my eyes there is nothing, absolutely nothing He can't fix in this world or beyond.

Seeing Him in that fragile state, I woke up with tears in my eyes and a splitting headache. Jumping out of bed, I shot a quick email to ask Swamiji if He was doing okay. Something didn't feel right. I waited and waited, and no reply came. Finally, just when I had given up, He wrote in. It's rare for Him to write a long email, but on this occasion, it was a long one. Probably because I needed to read this to understand what it takes to fix something. Here:

Dear Bhikkuram,

You see, finding Euro took some amount of energy because it was not just finding him but also aligning millions of other things.

Euro was not supposed to come back to the lady. He would have gone to a new owner and would have been quite happy there too. He would have gotten used to it in a matter of days. Dogs are never attached to their masters the way humans are attached to their people and pets. Dogs don't worry about the future or brood over the past. They have no ego. Absolutely no ego at all. So, they love back whoever offers them love and food.

By merely leaving a message in the universe, we could have created the possibility of bringing him back. But it would have taken a minimum of seven days. That's why I'd written that his chances of coming back were dim. Had Euro gone to the new owner, he would have fed Euro. Some of his resources were allocated to Euro. But now, where do we allocate those resources? The amount of food Euro would have consumed there throughout his time lasting a few years would be equivalent of that man's three month's salary. Now, he'll be out of a job for 3 months.

That was the only way to balance it. But I didn't want him out of a job right away. So, he would be between jobs for a period of three months.

The lady who owns Euro would have got a new pet in due course. This would have happened within four months had we not done absolutely anything about it. Or had I simply left a thought in the universe, it would have taken seven days minimum. Now, from where do we arrange four months' worth of food for Euro? (Because after 4 months the new pet would have balanced it out). To arrange for it, some resources had to be tilted in her direction. And the excess got consumed by people who attended her langar yesterday. Besides, losing Euro was simply a payback of her own karma but that had to be waived off by giving her something (sending back Euro) that just wasn't there in her bhagya, fate.

I intervened not purely out of compassion but out of care too. When I read that you were deeply disturbed, I felt I should step up and do whatever I could.

The new place where Euro would have shed his hair, left bones after eating meat (his new owner would have fed him meat) etc. was going to be the food of billions of microorganisms.

Alternative arrangements had to be made for them. Since you also made a request for intervention even after being a sannyasi and above all, my disciple, you became a party to the payment of the toll tax if you see what I mean. Since you'd made the request out of ignorance, compassion and empathy, and not out of any selfish motive, your suffering was limited to merely seeing a dream and waking up all jolted. Now, you won't actually have to see it in real life!

The only reason I shared this in brief detail is because I felt Nature wanted me to apprise you because as my disciple, there's much responsibility on your shoulders too. You are holding the baton of a guru, a lineage, that stands for extraordinary selflessness, surrender, devotion, tapas, dispassion.

In surrender, at the most we pray, but in our lineage, we never force Nature to act a certain way. If we must want Nature to be a certain way, then we must give it ample time so that things fall in their natural course. Almost all is possible in His world, but in His timeframe. And that timeframe is eternal. We can't really count it in hours, days, weeks or months. No one dies, no one is born. No one goes away, no one moves. It's all one big illusion. A trace of every living entity is present in every other. This is the body of Purushottam, Bhagavān.

Blessings,
Swami

Never have I since then asked Swamiji to ever heal anyone. It was an important lesson that all I had to do was leave an *arzi*, a request in His court. If it was meant to be, Mother Nature would fulfill it. The price of getting my own or someone else's wish fulfilled was too high.

I realized then that He was the one person who could actually bring change in this mad debilitating world. His pristine consciousness knew what was best for each one of us. I just had to trust in His wisdom. And my trust in Him, I may add, has been absolutely unshakeable from the very first moment, as has been the experience of countless others.

Moksha

Before death and liberation comes life, a lot of it. So, when I got a new life, new people came with it. Some I got on with, some I didn't, and many I came to appreciate over a period of time and vice versa. Not everyone has the grace for social niceties, or a soft speech and I had neither. It annoyed some and rightly so, for ashrams are not places for unsociable and reserved behavior. It makes people uncomfortable.

Every once in a while, some charitable persons took it upon themselves to apprise Swamiji of my aloof and distant conduct. In my defense, I never disrespected anyone or hurt their self-respect, not intentionally. Sri Hari is witness to that. I merely wanted a little space, as people with fragile mental health do. Not once in all of those four years did Swamiji ever pull me up. To anyone who had anything to say about me, He only defended me saying that I had a good heart and that everyone is built differently.

Some thought He was partial to me, for He never reprimanded me. And it didn't go unnoticed that my requests to Him were rarely denied.

What no one could muster the courage to ask Swamiji, I was pushed to ask. And I was happy because it was the truth. He never did rebuke me.

Once a lady passed a mean remark about me among a group of people and it reached my ears and His too. He always knows everything. It really upset me. I thought I wouldn't go to the ashram anymore; people can be so hurtful sometimes.

I remember so clearly what Swamiji had said to me, 'Many devotees will come and go. Often when their wishes are met, some will praise us, and some will keep it a secret. When their desires are not fulfilled some will leave, some will still come year after year for the love of God, but you, Bhikkuram, are here to stay. This is your home now.'

His kindness was that luminous light that kept me going, even when so often my mind found little joy in living. Also, the idea that there was something special about me was deeply rooted by now, for I did manage to get whether through appeals or tantrums both Swamiji's consideration and time. My special quality however turned out to be something so unexpected that never again did I ever entertain such an absurd idea about myself.

Here's how my delusion saw light. In 2017, Swamiji went into solitude from May until October. He stayed inside His cottage in the ashram seeing and speaking to no one.

Just before Swamiji completely slipped into solitude in May, as He was still finishing writing His blogposts for the next few months, I wrote Him an email regarding some publishing queries to be handled in His absence.

On the eve of 4th May, in Swamiji's response to one of my emails, was a line that read,

'Today's an important day, Bhikkuram, your mamma is finally liberated…she has attained *moksha*.'

I didn't understand what that meant. Swamiji had shown to me just last year mamma looking young and radiant. Where was she going now?

I actually nearly broke down, thinking, 'Had I lost my mother again?' With shaking hands, I wrote back to Swamiji asking what had happened. Swamiji apprised me that on His very first, and only, visit to my erstwhile home in Pune, something had unfolded. He wrote back:

> *Dear Sadhviji,*
>
> *The first time I met your mother was when I visited your home in Pune. It had been four months since her death, but unbeknownst to you, she was still in the house. Her spirit was unable to pass on because her attachment to you was immense. She worried about how you'd survive in this world.*
>
> *If you remember, I had asked you to give me ten minutes to rest up in the guest room, which had also been your mother's room when she was alive. Well, she was still in that room and wished to speak to me. All her life she had had myriad worldly desires, but they hadn't brought her any happiness. She didn't want that for you. She didn't ask me to help settle you down or get you married. It was your mamma's wish that as a saint, I take care of you. She said that when she was alive, she never visited any saints, maybe she should have.*
>
> *She further said to me, 'Dolly thinks she's quite shrewd and smart when in fact, she's naïve and foolish. And wouldn't survive in this cruel world, especially now that Sunny is set to work abroad.' You wouldn't last she said repeatedly.*

Mamma loved you deeply and her anxiety for your well-being stopped her from passing on. So, she made me promise her that I'll look after you.

Since that day I've tried my best to keep you safe and cared for. When it comes to you, one fundamental question I find myself asking is, 'If your parents were alive, what would they have done?'

In the course of our conversation, she also told me with much pride that you were an author and poet and how your books had been published by big publishers. She told me that if I could give you that seva, you would be really good at it.

Her love for you was so deep that she spoke to me not as a mother but as a soul asking me to take you with me.

Today her soul has finally been liberated and that's why she came today, to thank me. Unlike the last time, she didn't say anything, and simply smiled. She was at peace.

I didn't want to tell you this especially now when I'll be uncontactable for five months but since you asked me and I always speak the truth, so I wrote in.

Love and blessings,
Always watching over you,
Swami

Life humbles you, often cruelly, but in my case, love has humbled me. Swamiji's conscientious manner in which He had kept His words to my mother bewildered me. So many things of the past and the present made sense now. I felt such gratitude for my beautiful Guru, whose heart was tender like a child and who gave away everything He had for the happiness and comfort of others.

This incident also forever changed my outlook on death. No one was really dying, they were all there on the other side, in a prison of their making. Death was not a release as I had thought (and countless others think), it was merely another trap for the ones who didn't know how to live. I also now laughed at the idea of all those people seeking *moksha* in the other life.

It wasn't possible, not without achieving liberation from one's negative tendencies while alive.

This new knowledge and wisdom that I had discerned with Swamiji's grace, sparked in me a desire to share it with like-minded women. In time, the idea gave birth to the Women's Liberation Group (WLG) on Wildr.

Having seen how tough mamma's life had been, I realized that women were often neglected and neglect themselves even in the most supportive families. They spent their lives looking after everyone but never really took out the time to embark on their own spiritual quest until very late in life.

And the truth was that if anyone wanted to die in peace, then they had to work towards it. My whole idea of hankering after death went up in smoke, it was just another place where you felt helpless, even more so. This isn't how I had imagined embracing death. A lot changed in my mind that day.

Also, I felt a sense of deep awe for mamma and that a mother's affection can be so far-reaching and lasting, I could never have imagined. I had bid her goodbye a long time ago, scenes from after her cremation flashed in my mind. I had been so quick to cast her, her clothes, her belongings, off from our home...from my life because it hurt so much.

Our house had been so quiet, and none of us could ever go to mamma's room after her death. There seemed to be so much sadness in that room, which I attributed to her passing. How was I to know that in death as in life, she continued to suffer. It was very saddening to think that she was in the house all along, watching us grieve and struggle. But what about her? We couldn't have helped her at all.

God alone knows how long she would have stayed in that state if Swamiji hadn't come. I felt as if time was running out for me as well, I had to learn to live, truly live before I died, else nothing good would come from my passing either. I realized then, more than ever, that my Guru was my salvation. And death, that seemed like a sweet, peaceful sleep, was in reality a lengthy nightmare for the ignorant. It was hell. When I got over the initial shock and tears, I imagined what would have happened if Swamiji's holy feet had not found their way to our home. What would be my mother's and my fate?

The scriptures were right, only the holy ones could show the path to dharma and liberation. There was no other way.

It wasn't just Swamiji's might and power alone, but His pristine conduct and a rare humility only the most powerful can possess, in the face of disregard and affront that made Him Bhagavān to me. There's never been a time in the last ten years that I've been in distress and He hasn't answered my prayer. His omnipotence and omniscience are unquestionable to me, no matter how simple or human He appears to anyone.

A Blessing Given

While Swamiji was in solitude from May to September, many meaningful things transpired during that time. Someone I knew in the ashram, who was deeply devoted to Swamiji had a painful skin problem. The sores were springing up everywhere on the face. It wasn't that I had a big heart or something, I just thought if I can help I must.

So, one evening after the aarti, I took a pink hibiscus lying by Sri Hari's feet, said my Guru mantra on it and gave it to the person. I further added, 'Just as the pink hibiscus is, your skin will be beautiful once again.'

Nothing dramatic happened to the recipient of the blessing, but over the next few days the blood stopped oozing from the affected spots and the redness started to go down. There were blotch marks on the face still, but healing seemed to be underway. In a few months, the problem didn't completely disappear, but it appeared nothing more than acne compared to the agonizing breakout from before. However, after a few weeks, something strange happened to me. My entire forehead was covered with tiny acne.

Even as a teenager, I never had those issues. It was my brother who would be applying *Multani Mitti*, Fuller's Earth, to his cheeks trying to stub out a bout of acne. All my life I've had clear skin. It was quite intriguing that something like that should happen to me overnight.

One morning, I woke up with splotches of blood on my pillow. A few acne had burst. It also hurt very much. I immediately remembered the words of that person, how painful and bloody those gashes could get. I didn't want to believe that it was happening to me because I had used my Guru mantra not on some life-threatening sickness, but because I had felt bad on seeing someone's plight.

Swamiji had warned me in the past to not let my emotions get the better of me. And to use the sadhana where it was most needed, for there was always a price to pay. I wondered, if healing something as insignificant can cause such discomfort and pain then what about Swamiji who healed such grave diseases. But I already knew the answer.

I had only ever seen Him unwell with one thing after the other. The health troubles would keep changing but the bottom line was that He would be in pain and acute discomfort. That was the norm in His world.

I looked in the mirror and convinced myself it'd go away in a week or so, nearly four months passed by and it only got from bad to worse. Nothing seemed to work, no ointments, no medication. By now I had tried everything. One morning, Vidya Swami said to me looking at the pitiful state of my forehead, 'Why don't you apply *chandan*, sandal wood, it'll help.'

I thanked Vidya Swami for his brilliant idea. What I didn't tell him was that I had already tried applying *chandan* a few times and it hadn't helped. Surprisingly, that particular morning I had had a brilliant idea too. Anything that comes to me in my morning japa, I take it very seriously. I feel it's Sri Hari Himself who's telling me what to do. Now because I had used or misused my powers, mantra, I had to bear its consequences. And nothing worldly was going to cure it. Bhagavān alone could redeem me.

The only way was to apply the sandalwood, from Sri Hari's vigraha's holy feet to my forehead. And offer my karma at His feet. He alone could heal me. Later I thought maybe I'm being dramatic and silly. So, when Vidya Swami too spoke of *chandan* that morning, I thought maybe it's a sign. *He is also a great sadhak, I should at least honor his word, especially, after assuring him that I'd do as he had told.*

Next day, I applied the *chandan* from Bhagavān's feet on my forehead. By the next day itself, all those painful bumps had started to recede like waves in low tide. I was so blown away. A day, that's all it took for something I was struggling with for months!

Since then, I always rub the *chandan* from Bhagavān's feet on my forehead. It's Sri Hari's loving grace I wear on my forehead each morning, out of love, out of gratitude. Also, the person in question whom I had used the mantra on, does have an unmistakable soft pink hue on the face like the hibiscus, as I had said.

In July, the graceful Matarani visited the ashram for Guru Poornima. A woman of extraordinary gentleness, much like her saintly son. It's no surprise that Matarani's loving mannerisms can be seen in Swamiji. She had come along with the beautiful Didi and her doting husband, Suvinder Gargas, who shares an equally deep bond with Swamiji. They couldn't have Swamiji's darshan, but it was enough for them to feel His energy, which was quite palpable. There was a serenity in the ashram air, the sky seemed subdued and the general atmosphere calm.

When it wasn't raining heavily, it was misty and dewy, as if a piece of heaven was floating on earth. It was a peaceful time in many ways, yet it was also filled with inner turmoil and battles for the handful present in the ashram.

Since there were only a limited number of cottages back then, and all occupied, it had always happened in the past that Didi and I shared a room, Matarani and Suvi bhaiya stayed in the next one. During this time, I had a six-month long sadhana going on, and at such a time no one could stay with me.

Such were Swamiji's instructions. But when the three of them arrived, I felt quite fretful that they'll have to share one small room, while I had an entire room to myself. It didn't feel right, as everyone had to wake up for the morning aarti.

I wrote a note to Swamiji and left it on His lunch tray. The next day written in perfect cursive handwriting came a note from Him.

Dear Bhikkuram,

Sure, Didi can stay with you for the next few days. Re your sadhana, simply keep a bowl of soaked rice in a corner in your room.

Also, staying together will be good for both of you. It'll give you a chance to mend and reconnect.

Blessings,
Swami

I read the note, and the ground beneath my feet shifted. Didi and I had been a little distant due to some odd misunderstanding a couple of months back. Neither of us had mentioned a word to Swamiji. He knew about it anyway. I showed that note to Didi and she laughed saying, 'We just can't hide anything from Him, ever.'

Things went back to normal after that and as usual Didi and I spent some cozy nights reminiscing about Swamiji. She's very childlike and looking at her always gives me a feeling that I'm looking at Swamiji. I've always had a high regard for her, and she has always treated me with great love and respect.

It so happened that Matarani and Didi were taking their afternoon tea and we were all chatting up when I remembered a vivid dream I had recently had.

'Maa, I had a dream where you wanted me to meet someone. You were quite insistent.'

A motherly smile flashed on her face as she sipped her tea. In all those years, I had only ever seen her smile. Her speech, tender like her son's, could disarm anyone.

'Tell me, Sadhviji, what did you see?'

'There was a tall, formidable man standing next to you. He wore a white bushirt, black trousers, and had an old-style trunk in his hand. It felt as if he was off to drop you to a bus-station or something like that. I had a strange sense in the dream that he was related to you...but you are so fair, Maa and he was dark-complexioned, hair parted to the side, I think.'

'Mamaji,' Didi said looking at Matarani, who mumbled, '*Bhappa*,' which is how she had always addressed her elder brother.

'In my dream you kept insisting that I had to leave everything I was doing and meet him first.'

It was very astonishing to hear that I had dreamt of Swamiji's Uncle, the great Shiva *bhakta*, who was also His first Guru. He had initiated Swamiji at the age of fourteen with the consecrated holy ash from cremation grounds.

Mysterious are the ways of the universe. I don't know what it meant and there was no way of asking Swamiji right away, but something in my heart said that it was some kind of sign that he had come to see if I was up to the task.

For I had never spoken about him, let alone seen a picture to know what he looked like. I never dreamt of him again, but the uncanny and vivid dream left a strange impression on me.

For by now, I knew that people on the other side were well and alive. The ones who knew how to yoke their consciousness to Bhagavān, neither space nor time could bind them. They were the awakened ones.

Swamiji had shown me that with my Mother, a life without Bhagavān in it was only endless suffering, there was no peace for them even in death. As for the awakened, realized souls, they were free from birth, death and decay.

Making an offering during Guru Purnima celebrations, at Swamiji's paduka, while He's away in solitude.

A smiling Swamiji, along with His devoted disciples, Swami Vidyananda and Sadhvi Shraddha, listening to a bhajan a devotee is singing, particularly for Swamiji.

Swamiji's silent and mystical gaze as He looks on, while a group of devotees give a beautiful musical performance.

The book launch of *The Legend of the Goddess* (2024). A monumental moment when Swamiji appreciated my editorial skills.

Devotees gathered in London to have Swamiji's holy darshan as He walks amidst the crowd like a shining Sun.

Doing the Kinhin meditation at the Golden Palms in Bangalore and sporting a pleased look for leading the ladies.

Swamiji's grace giving blessed hands raised high to call out *Jai Kara: Bolo Sri Hari Bhagavān ki Jai!*

The beautiful and powerful Lord stands silent and ever-watchful, fulfilling His devotees' wishes and protecting them from the storms of their own karma.

In the early days after Sanyasa diksha, a newbie Sanyasi.

Basking in Swamiji's divine humor during a discourse.

The mesmerizing halo and Srivatsa mark that appeared on Swamiji's photo on Krishna Janmashtami.

Birthday blessings on my 38th at the Gayatri Sadhana retreat in Bangalore.

Swamiji's loving and kind smile that time and again steals the heart of the young and the old, lost and the ailing.

The lovely Matarani, with a heart of gold and a mind so practical, pure and utterly beautiful.

Early days of Kitchen Seva, smeared in haldi and grease from the stove.

Swamiji's kind, laughing eyes are like a balm to His devotees.

Sitting by the lotus feet of Sri Hari while listening to Swamiji's discourse in rapt attention.

In Bhagavān's service with love and deep devotion, Sadhvi Shraddha and myself.

Sanyasis and Brahmacharis surrounding beloved Om Swamiji, our loving Guru and Bhagavān.

Divine Darshan

In the months that went by, preparing Swamiji's lunch and sometimes dropping in a note, a cute cartoon, or a joke book were the little things Vidya Swami and I looked forward to. I felt that if Swamiji was reading jokes and anecdotes, then He won't perhaps be too serious as He is when He is all by Himself.

We couldn't see Him, but His divine presence was unmistakable. In our small world, we were simply happy to serve Him. I've to admit here that I was a bit sly and had found a little crack in the blind of His study. In the evening, when Swamiji turned on the lights of His study and went downstairs to fetch His supper tray at around 5.15–5.30 pm, for a fraction of a second I'd get a glimpse of a swish of His clothes from above the high-ground behind His cottage.

Some days, on my way back from listening to Lalita Sahasranama in the temple, I'd stand there just to see that shadow. As the months rolled on, my heart just knew that Swamiji's energy was different, softer, gentler, as if a different person lived in the cottage now.

I even dragged Didi to catch a glimpse of Swamiji around Guru Purnima. We had barely waited five minutes when I had excitedly said, 'Didi, there He is!'

'Where? I see no one, Sadhviji…I'm a bit scared, I don't like annoying Swamiji. And He'll be if He sees us huddled here.'

'Just wait, Didi, we aren't disobeying any guidelines. We are just standing outside taking in the ashram air.'

A couple of minutes later, clutching Didi's arm lightly, I said, 'Look now, do you see?'

'I think…I saw a movement,' she said a little puzzled waiting to see more.

'Great then, show is over. We can see this again tomorrow, if you like.'

'Thank you, Sadhviji, but I think this is enough for me,' she responded, smiling cutely.

Soon it was time for Matarani and Didi to leave. They are so much like Swamiji that parting from them can feel like you've lost a bit of Swamiji when they aren't around. But they had to go back home as Pitashree, Swamiji's much loved father was all by himself. I had met him on a few occasions, and he had been very kind, addressing me sometimes as 'the Colonel's daughter'. An endearment that totally endeared him to me.

His vast knowledge of Indian history, our rich political backdrop, constitution, judiciary and practically every other act passed by the Indian Government since and before Independence made my head swirl. I thought no wonder Swamiji's a guzzler of information. Both of Swamiji's parents were exceptional people, and none more capable of nurturing the extraordinary child that was born to them. In fact, a beautiful tale from Swamiji's childhood just goes to show how extraordinary indeed.

Once Maa was invited to a wedding in their neighbourhood. She had known the lady for a long time now. Her husband worked in Kashmir while she undertook some odd sewing jobs to raise her children. It was her eldest daughter's wedding. The groom and his family had arrived and had been waiting a while but there was no sign of the Panditji who had been invited to conduct the ceremony.

The girl's mother was getting nervous. There wasn't much of a dowry and now with this delay, who knows what would happen if the Panditji didn't come. Matarani understood the gravity of the situation and hurried back home to the one person who could help her no matter what the problem.

Swamiji engrossed in reading a book, was quick to see that Matarani seemed worried. She asked her son, was it possible for Him to marry the young couple next door, chant the holy mantras and declare them married. Not one to deny His mother, He left with her immediately for the girl's house.

To the surprise of all present, the young boy of twelve recited the holy chants perfectly in His spell-binding voice. He concluded the ceremony which lasted nearly an hour in the *vidhipoorvak*, ritualistic manner prescribed in the Vedas. Midway through the ceremony the Panditji arrived. He couldn't help but marvel at the accuracy with which Swamiji was performing the ceremony.

He said to Maa, 'I'm confident that you must have read the Bhagavatam for such an erudite boy to have been born to you.'

After Matarani left, the ashram felt a little empty, but I always had my secret spot to have Swamiji's darshan.

Each day, just sensing that little flash of a movement filled me with such joy. Afterwards, I'd always offer my pranams by touching my forehead to the ground. I loved the feeling of revering Swamiji from afar, especially after how He had saved mamma, something inside me had totally dissolved.

There were no doubts in my head ever after that. I may have had my little battles with Him inside my head, but every last trace of skepticism I had harbored was long gone. It obviously changed me at a deeper level, stirring a desire to be a good and kinder human being. His compassion had set the benchmark so high, the only thing I could do was emulate Him.

Towards the beginning of September, I waited outside the study window. On that particular day, I felt His shadow to be closing in. Before I knew, the blind had been pulled down tightly. It looked like I had been found out. The crack was closed for good now, no more peeping I thought. At least the Divine had allowed me this indulgence for a little while. In that briefest of time, I had caught a glimpse of a sort of *abha*, a red hue that my mind couldn't just dismiss. It was more knowing than seeing that it was Mother Divine Herself who had come to the window just now.

I sensed as if His soft and gentle countenance was not of a man but a woman. I remember falling to my knees and offering my pranams to Him and the Divine Mother right there on the ground. A day later, with the meal tray came a signed publishing contract and a bunch of A4 sheets. I picked one of the sheets and realized that it was a beautiful pencil drawing of the Divine Mother! Oh, it was breathtaking. Written underneath was one word – *Mother.*

Exactly three days later came another set of A4 sheets and in there was the most exquisite drawing of a resting Lord Narayana. It was so intricately done that I couldn't help but wonder how long it must have taken to draw Bhagavān. On the top right side of the drawing these words were penciled in – *The only truth. Eternal. Ever beautiful.*

The day He stepped out of His solitude, a handful of us were gathered. Matarani too had returned for Her son, Guru and Bhagavān's darshan. He has always been all three to her.

To me, on that auspicious day, He appeared to have transformed into a gentle, loving Mother himself. The Swamiji whom we had bid farewell in April was different from the one who sat in front of us five months later. His beard and hair had grown all jet black, yet, the Chandan and Kumkum tilak, especially the Kumkum gave Him a very soft, feminine and tender appearance. It was déjà vu all over again. I may have sensed the reddish hue of His radiance from outside, but actually seeing Him was like being in the presence of the Divine Mother. When He played the Shiv Tandav on the piano for everyone, I cried hard like my lost precious treasure was being returned to me. I remember we fed Him bell-pepper pasta for lunch. Vidya Swami and I had literally danced all the way from the kitchen to the study carrying Swamiji's food tray. We kept staring at Him as He ate His meal as if afraid that He might disappear again.

pitāsi lokasya carācarasya
tvamasya pūjyaśca gururgarīyān |
na tvatsamo 'styabhyadhikaḥ kuto 'nyo
lokatraye 'pyapratimaprabhāva ||43||

You are the father of this universe, of all things, moving and non-moving. You are the greatest of the Gurus (preceptor) and worthy of worship. There is none equal to You in the three worlds. Your power is unequalled! How can anyone be greater than You?

Bhagavad Gita, 11.43.

2018

Lump It

In the month of April, the Ram Katha was hosted in the ashram, a seven-day affair concluding on Sri Hari's birthday. For five beautiful days the event went on. The wonderful *kirtan-mandali* sang beautiful bhajans, when the main Panditji, Kathavachak, storyteller would take a small break from regaling us with stories of Lord Rama. Panditji was a man in his early fifties with a mop of curly hair. He was full of anecdotes to help the audience better understand the life of Lord Rama. I sat on the Garbhagriha stairs where I always sit, fanning myself as it was a hot April month. It's been kind of my spot since after initiation, as it allowed me to look both at Swamiji and Sri Hari unabashedly.

On one of the days Panditji narrated Princess Sita's marriage to Prince Rama. Panditji then cracked some joke about modern day relationships and how the husbands can't wait to get away from their wives and vice-versa. Panditji sounded so like Swamiji, for his views on love and marriage were quite the same that I turned to look at Sri Hari. He looked resplendent draped in fine silk *vastras*, heavily garlanded and with a naughty smile on His lips.

I said to Him, 'You must be quite enjoying yourself.' I stared at His pointy ears thinking that everything Sri Hari knew Swamiji was privy to. 'Those fine antennas on your ears, must tell you everything.'

I hadn't even had the time to blink when something came flying at me, hitting me on my shoulder. It stung me and I went 'ow'. On closer inspection the object to hit me was a marigold flower, but my God, did it sting. The speed with which the flower had come at me was so dramatic that those seated in the front row too were startled. Some came and joked about it later.

The next day again during the Katha, a flower fell in my lap, and I cupped it in my palms, thinking that wow Bhagavān's really hitting me with all these flowers. Two days later, during Swamiji's evening discourse, a marigold from a row of flowers from the decoration fell near my hand. I was about to pick it up, thinking Bhagavān has sent me more love, but cast aside that thought as being stupid and impractical.

> *If every fallen flower was from Bhagavān then I'd be picking up flowers the whole day. I'm imagining things, since I'm so good at it.*

Right at that moment, mid-way during His discourse, Swamiji paused and, without turning back He very quietly said, '*Sadhviji, ye aashish hai apke liye, this is a blessing for you.*' His hand raised mid-air in a blessing. I was stunned. It doesn't matter how many times, Swamiji is able to read your thoughts, each time it happens it shakes you a little.

What never occurred to me was that there was a reason Bhagavān was piling me up with so many blessings.

Soon enough, life took a different turn, as I discovered that there was a knot, the size of a pea in my armpit. What was worrisome was that it wasn't on the outside of the skin but inside it. It wasn't painful so I didn't pay much attention until, I started to feel a heaviness in my left side running from my shoulder to my hand.

It got to a point that at all times, I had an awareness I was lugging my arm around. It was a strange feeling, like carrying an appendage. I knew something was wrong because on the surface everything seemed alright. It was a foreboding feeling that nothing good is going to come of this.

It was summer in the ashram, and it became quite uncomfortable in the heat to have that left arm in a fitting armhole of my robes. I began ripping the left sleeve of my robes to make it comfier and to avoid any friction between the knot and the cotton cloth. Fortunately, the absurdity of ripping one arm of my robes wasn't visible as it got covered by the *angvastram* on top. I even spoke to a couple of doctor friends, who suggested some antibiotics.

The medicines didn't do much, and I just learnt to adjust with this new arrangement of knowing that I had a touchy left arm.

My long sadhana was going on and I stayed put in the ashram for the next few months. By the time October came, the soft knot in the armpit had turned into a hard lump. Even an idiot could tell it wasn't a good sign. I was scared internally but didn't know how to deal with it. I didn't wish to bother Swamiji in His solitude.

By the time He returned to the ashram in October, things weren't going great for me. Finally, I mentioned about the heaviness in my arm.

'Even in my sleep I can feel its weight. It's the oddest sensation, Swamiji.'

He gently scolded me for not telling Him earlier and not visiting a doctor. The somber look on His face confirmed any doubts that I may have had that there was something terribly wrong indeed. My fear must have shown on my face as I sat near Swamiji's feet, because He soon asked Vidya Swami to step out of the study for a few minutes. Placing His hand on my head, He spoke in a deep timbre. It was a *sabar* mantra and He told me that He rarely ever asked Divine Mother for healing.

He then asked me to get an appointment to see a good doctor and get an ultrasound done. Everything moved very quickly from there and a couple of days later, the ultrasound report came in. It read that the mass seemed to be benign. 'Maa has healed you,' He said.

'Is this what you meant in 2016 when you said in a different life, I'd have had to undergo long chemo sessions, Swamiji?'

'Lymphoma, cancer of the lymph nodes, is what it's called,' He said nodding, 'but there's nothing to worry about now, Bhikkuram, all's well with Her grace.'

The heaviness and pain in my arm took a few months to disappear. I can still feel the discomfort sometimes but mostly it's fine.

It flared up again four years later in June 2023, as I was writing this book. This time there was a bigger lump and swelling that just couldn't be ignored. A rushed ultrasound and full blood work later, it turned out the mass had grown. This time Swamiji wasn't in India but when has that ever stopped Him from healing a person.

Once again, Swamiji reassured me that there was nothing to worry about. But I wasn't so sure. It looked really bad. This time the scare was worse, the growth had spread to other lymph nodes. A concern equally reflected in the loving and grave manner in which Dr Geeta Baro, (the ashram's remarkable resident doctor) did the initial check-up and asked me to get an ultrasound without a moment's delay.

In those three-four days I tried to wrap up my affairs, at least mentally. I wasn't unhappy altogether, the only thing that surprised me was this great, heavy sadness that I experienced from being parted from Swamiji. To not be able to see Him again, at least in this life.

But as the solemn power of Swamiji's words, once again, the growth turned out to be benign. And as He had predicted, with medication it became better. Benign or not, the only thing I'm certain about is that it was His grace alone that had saved me yet again.

Back to 2018, by the time the year ended, after the initial knot episode, my hair had started to fall gradually at first, then in clumps, especially from the top and the sides. Didi was the first one to notice and insisted that we take this seriously. I hadn't shed a single tear in front of Swamiji when I had that lump in my armpit. But when it came to my hair, my eyes had welled up of their own accord. He lovingly but firmly said that I must eat well, have supplements, massage my scalp and wait, in time it'll be alright. There was no other cure for it. He had very cutely pointed out to the crown on his head, 'If there was some spiritual remedy for it, don't you think I'd have saved my own hair.'

That made both of us laugh. When I was on my own though, it was no laughing matter. I was distraught. My scalp had begun to show from the sides, one could see the scalp through my thinning hair. It broke me in a way nothing in life had. It felt like a great punishment had been meted out to me. I felt very alone, lost, and certain that my hair was never coming back. Everyone took my worries lightly, but the mirror spoke the truth. One evening, I went to Sri Hari and said through a haze of tears, 'If you are okay with me looking like this, then I'm okay looking this way.' Bhagavān's eyes brimming with love, brought me peace and an acceptance that I didn't think was possible so soon. He does that, you know, sets you on a different path without you ever noticing, until you are well on your way to a different destination.

Deep End

A month after my initiation, in 2016, was an ashram event. To my utter surprise, Swamiji had asked me to hold meditation sessions in the mornings.

I was flabbergasted. 'But I've never conducted a meditation session let alone done it myself properly.'

'Don't worry, you'll be fine. I'll be there,' He said.

That had brought me relief momentarily until I realized He meant spiritually present and not physically. Three days passed and Swamiji had been so occupied with meetings that He had no time to spare. And in all probability, He had forgotten all about it. But like a fishbone in my throat, I hadn't, especially when the first session was scheduled for the next morning. I could no longer show restraint and asked Him to give me at least half an hour to explain how to go about conducting the session.

'Ten minutes is all you need.' Grinning, Swamiji put aside His laptop. 'You should do a *stuti*, Bhikkuram, in the beginning of the session.'

'I only know one *stuti*, Swamiji, Guru Bramha, Guru Vishnu...'

With the kindest smile He said to me, 'Fine, you just do this *stuti* and I'll show up for you.'

The next morning in the temple, I did exactly as I had been asked to.

'How did it go?' Swamiji asked me at lunch.

'People were crying so I think it went well, I cried too. Although, some thought, I was crying in devotion.'

'You weren't?' He expressed surprise and was as usual amused with my response.

'No, I was just sad.'

That became the benchmark - if people felt moved by my session, then it was a successful one. And such is my benevolent Guru's grace that as time passed, I cried out of sheer devotion as we would visualize playing with Lord Narayana or sitting in the lap of the Divine Mother.

Wherever my heart took me, and whatever words Sri Hari, standing behind me in the temple, whispered in my head, I blurted out without a second thought. And it moved people deeply, and continues to do so, for those are His words; I'm merely the mouth, repeating them. They stood behind me, the Supreme Lord Narayana and the Devi Lakshmi, silently smiling, showering their love. This has been Swamiji's greatest blessing to me, the love of Sri Hari. Without His grace I'd never know how or what it is to meditate on the Divine Lord.

For a long time, Swamiji would ask me after every meditation session, 'How did it go?' and my replies would always amuse Him, especially when I'd say things such as, 'We played in Mother Divine's garden,' or 'Bhagavān swung us around in the air like little children,' or 'We went to Vaikuntha today,' or 'We experienced dying,' and so on.

It also became a tradition of sorts that on the last day of the event, I'd narrate a mystical anecdote of Swamiji that had recently transpired. I had just returned from the city when I heard about the village lady, Rati (name changed) who was bitten by a poisonous Blue Krait. The snake is highly venomous and if the person is left untreated, the poison can be fatal. I had known Rati since I first arrived to live in the ashram in 2014.

In the four years that I had known her, she had led a very unhappy life. Living with a physically abusive and lazy husband was hellish. She had four young children to feed.

She was barely managing to pull together when she lost her baby to a kitchen fire. It was too much to bear. She started to experience severe bouts of depression, so much so that she had to be moved to her mother's place to recuperate. If all this wasn't enough, a year later, one of the bulls in her yard rammed a big horn in her thigh, causing serious damage.

There was no hospital nearby and to travel to find treatment was a painful affair. I had not met a woman who suffered as much at the hands of fate as she did. Her only solace was seeing Swamiji and doing some seva in the ashram, which was also forbidden by her husband. Fearful of his lashings she'd sneak out when she could. She'd always say to me, 'Please pray for me to Swamiji. He's my only hope.'

So, when I heard in 2018 that Rati had been bitten by a snake, I almost felt relieved for her that maybe this was her chance to be free of the snares of the vicious world. In the evening, over dinner, when I apprised Swamiji about Rati's condition, all He said was, 'Hmm.'

'Swamiji, please release Rati from her suffering... please help her pass on.'

Alarmed He spoke, 'Bhikkuram, she has young children, who'll look after them?'

'Swamiji, she's so unhappy all the time, I thought...'

Swamiji smiled and said, 'Unlike you, not everyone who's unhappy wants to die. The children need their mother and I need to save her, if it isn't already too late.'

The next day, the news came that Rati made a miraculous recovery. Later, I heard from her friend, Sumitra, who also worked in the ashram about the events that led up to her revival. In Sumitra's words, 'Where do I even begin...Rati was admitted to the ICU and was put on a ventilator. She was unconscious and unresponsive for over 24 hours. It didn't look like she was going to make it; the poison had spread deep.'

Sumitra had appealed for a personal meeting with Swamiji, and as soon as she saw Him, she burst into tears pleading with Him to save her friend's life. He had heard her patiently but remained quiet for a wee bit. He then said, 'I can't promise anything now, it's a fatal bite but with Bhagavān's grace anything is possible.'

He asked Sumitra that His name (Om Swami) be whispered in Rati's ears like a chant, for an hour at the hospital. It'd be enough time to know if she'd be able to make it or not. Rati's brother-in-law was by her side in the hospital shift, and he did exactly as advised.

To the shock and surprise of everyone, within the hour, Rati regained consciousness and made it out of the hospital soon enough.

A few days later, when I had met a recovered Rati on the ashram grounds, I was astonished see how hale and hearty she seemed. I thanked Swamiji for making her well and not listening to my plea of a send-off to a better place, to which Swamiji replied, 'Bhikkuram where do you find such empathy in your heart?'

On one such day in October 2018, as usual Swamiji asked me post lunch about the morning meditation session. Since we always have new people coming to the ashram after reading Swamiji's books, sometimes a few end up skipping the meditation session to go down to the river or bask in the morning sun or would rather have their fill of breakfast.

'People were less but the session was nice…a few did cry, so all in all good, Swamiji.'

'Why were there less people?'

'Swamiji, less is great because then it's a like-minded bunch. It's just that sometimes it can be difficult with larger numbers, as some like getting up in the middle of the session, opening the door (which creaks loudly) and disturbing everyone else who's deep into meditation by then. We make announcements beforehand, to turn off the phone, please don't leave in the middle of the session and so on, but it doesn't make much of a difference. They do what they have to do,' I laughed a bit exasperated.

In the evening, Swamiji came to the temple. Mid-way through the discourse, a teasing smile on His face, Swamiji made an announcement that He had a surprise for a handful of special people. I was as intrigued as everyone else. He then made us all even more curious by saying we'd have to wait until the end of the discourse to hear it.

Towards the end of the discourse, Swamiji made various announcements, but not a mention of the surprise. A devotee spoke up, 'Swamiji, you haven't told us what the surprise is.'

'I'm not done yet,' He said, showing His beautiful, even white teeth.

At last, Swamiji asked, 'All those who had attended Sadhviji's meditation session this morning, please raise your hands.'

Quite a few hands went up and just as many didn't.

Swamiji cast a compelling glance around the temple, 'Those who attended the meditation session in the morning, I am giving you all a very special blessing today.'

A cheer went through the crowd, this was indeed a surprise! I was just as taken aback by Swamiji's magnanimity. Swamiji continued in His deep and powerful voice, 'I'm not going to tell you what the blessing is, but it's special. And in time, you'll know it.'

Before the year ended, I had a dream of Maa, only it wasn't a dream. I don't know what name to give Her form, just that She was the highest form in existence for She appeared on Her throne, with tall arches high above Her golden asana. She wasn't an image, a manifestation or conjecture of my mind. It was as if She was allowing me a glimpse of where She sat in all Her majesty.

Just as the *Viraat Swaroopa*, She was so huge, there was nothing left to see behind, beyond, or next to Her ornamented as an empress, clad in red and bejeweled with molten gold, She was regal, magnificent, tall and more mesmerizing than words can say. Her face I couldn't see, how could I have? How can one take in Her beauty, that mind-numbing radiance? It wasn't for a mere mortal like me to see.

The whole thing lasted less than thirty seconds, and She was gone. Before She left, my hands had come together of their own accord above my head, just as they had when Sri Hari appeared in 2015. In that fraction of a moment, I offered Her my salutations. Who was She, I don't know, but it felt like She was the Goddess who was Mother to all the other Goddesses.

I don't know why Maa came. I hadn't done anything to deserve Her presence, except calling out to Her in sorrow the last few years. But what I did know in my bones is that She had come at Swamiji's behest, by His blessings alone.

mayyāveśya mano ye māṁ nityayuktā upāsate |
śraddhayā parayopetāḥ te me yuktatamā matāḥ ||2||

Those whose minds are ever united with Me in worship,
are filled with ultimate faith, and are absorbed in me.
I consider them to be the most devoted to me.

Bhagavad Gita, 12.2.

2019

In One Stroke

Sometimes, just as a car on a country road, life keeps hitting bumps one after the other, 2019 was a bumpy ride for me. Try as I may, I just couldn't seem to find my bearings. It wasn't just the alarming hair loss, mentally too, it felt like I was regressing.

Around mid-February, I just walked into a salon and sat on the hairdresser's chair.

'Please cut my hair short, leave one inch on top and no more.'

'Just one inch?' the guy nervously asked, certain that I'll be at his throat if he cut it that short.

'Don't worry, just do it and dare you try and style it.' I glared at him. I then closed my eyes and just let go. The new haircut was a whole lot more skin and hair, like freshly mowed blades of grass. When I reached home looking like a cancer patient, Deepa got very upset and couldn't stop crying, 'Sadhviji…'

A few days later, when I got to the ashram, neither Swamiji nor Vidya Swami could hide their unhappiness on seeing me like that. Their way of showing their affection and support was different though.

'Now you look like a real Bhikku, monk. Reminds me of Pema Chodron, the famous American Tibetan-Buddhist nun. This suits you, Bhikkuram, it suits you,' Swamiji said.

In his Kannada-accented English, Vidya Swami exclaimed, 'What a haircut, hundred marks.' Vidya Swami would always look at my hair and say, 'It's not that your hair is less, it's just silky.' This line never failed to make me laugh, so he'd say it every other day, different variations of it like, 'Wow, see how fine your hair is growing back, it's like a dense forest now,' So, while I had all the support I needed, there were also curiosities to satisfy.

Some thought I had cut my hair because of some mental issues, others thought I shouldn't have cut my hair, and then some thought it looked really cool. There was plenty of advice flying left, right and center at me.

Someone asked me, 'How does it feel?'

'I feel liberated.'

It was the truth. My vanity, the outlook associated with looking a certain way, had been crushed so badly that with this episode I no longer cared how I appeared.

Over the next few weeks, months, quite a few ashram residents and devotees followed suit, creating this wave of shaved female heads. Someone said to me, 'Sadhviji, you are quite the trendsetter.'

Another person said, 'It looks so cool on you that everyone's following suit.'

The price for setting the trend was too high though. While others did it out of choice, I had had none. I shared with Swamiji and Vidya Swami how my new haircut was all the rage. Both were quite amused that from being on the verge of despair and bald headedness, I had gone on to be a trendsetter. Bhagavān had turned my loss (hair-loss) literally into a little victory in one stroke, and life carried on, business as before.

Chapati

Once it so happened that I had to make chapatis for Swamiji. I can cook almost anything now with His grace, but when it comes to making nice fluffy chapatis, everything fails. If there's one kitchen nightmare I have, it's making chapatis. Vidya Swami and Vidu Swami had to go to the city to file their visa applications. They were to travel with their Guru to a few international destinations in summer, and the visas had to be filed in advance. On that particular day, it was down to me to serve Swamiji a hot lunch. I've always found making chapatis very stressful, and this day was no different. A chapati was like an onion to me; it could make me cry. I constantly missed Vidya Swami as he was the chapati expert.

None of my chapatis came out right, and with great stress and anxiety, I served Swamiji His meal, with a chapati as flat as a crisp. The following one wasn't any better. I thought I'd burst into tears any minute when He said to me, 'The chapatis are nice. I'm eating them, aren't I?'

Mentally, I thought, 'Of course, you'd eat them. You are so kind that if I were to serve pebbles, you'd have them too.'

Without lifting His head from the plate, He said, 'Well, not that kind.'

I rushed out of there as fast as I could to tackle the next chapati, which came out like a crunchy papadam. I prayed to the Divine Mother to at least let one chapati fluff up. Swamiji's meal was almost over as I served Him the third disappointing chapati. Seeing me so stressed out and upset, He gazed at the flat chapati I was holding and made a gesture with His hands, saying, '*Ja*, go.'

I couldn't understand what He meant. There was finality, a command in the gesture, but its meaning completely eluded me. I was too tense to make sense of anything.

As I put the last chapati on the tawa, to my utter surprise, it started to rise as soon as the sides had been cooked. It fluffed up without a fuss, on its own. I hadn't even given it any gentle nudges yet, and it was round and fat, its belly swelling on the tawa. I could only gape at the effortlessness with which the perfectly round and fluffy chapati had turned out. I excitedly ran back with the latest offering.

'Swamiji, look, it's so fluffy,' I stuttered.

Swamiji smiled and said, 'Happy now?'

Looking back, I can say with certainty that this business with the chapati had mystified me even more than the other hair-raising feats I've seen Swamiji do. To have such authority over the nature of things, tangible and intangible, so as to command them to change their course at such a micro level was beyond my comprehension. Try as I may, I couldn't make sense of the mysterious forces that were at His beck and call. For how could one possibly make a chapati rise in the world simply by commanding it so?

Vidya Swami once confided in me, swearing me to secrecy that I'd never share this with anyone, that the Divine Mother's nine companion energies surrounded his Guru at all times. Little did he know that one day, I'd put it in a book for the whole world to read! It's true I really can't keep secrets; it's not there in my DNA.

In 2012, it'd been a year since Swamiji's vision of the Divine Mother. He had settled in the ashram, in the mud hut with only Vidya Swami and Raghu Swami to look after Him. A saint living by the river with His two disciples, it's all the ashram comprised of. Those were, as Vidya Swami likes to recall, his 'golden days'.

In those days, Swamiji's samadhi, meditative state, was extremely deep, and by simply speaking of the Goddess, He'd slip into a trance. In one such moment of equipoise, Vidya Swami posed a question to Swamiji regarding the Dashamahavidya, the *vidya* of awakening the ten Goddesses, the various aspects of the Divine Mother, from the most fearsome and fierce Kali to the most gentle and benevolent, Maa Kamakshi or Kamalatmika.

'Bauji, how long does it take to awaken one form of the Goddess?'

He remained silent for a while, and Vidya Swami thought Swamiji wasn't going to answer at all. And then, in His deep voice, Swamiji spoke, 'It can take lifetimes for someone to awaken the Dashamahavidya. Even the most illustrious and noble of saints have only awakened one Dashamahavidya in a lifetime. Sri Ramakrishna Paramahamsa, for instance, awakened the Goddess Kali.'

'Please forgive me my insolence but whom have you awakened, Bauji?' Vidya Swami asked hands folded, a little afraid to displease his master.

Smiling at Vidya Swami's question, Swamiji replied, 'One can't reach Jagdamba, the Mother Goddess without awakening all Her different aspects.'

Vidya Swami's jaw had dropped open as Swamiji continued, '*Aapke Swami ne saari Dashamahavdiya siddh ki hain,* your Swami has awakened all the Dashamahavidyas.'

Never before and never after that day did Swamiji ever utter those words again, but hearing it from His mouth once was enough to instill both fear and awe in Vidya Swami. This story was then passed on to me a few years later, and I've until now kept it a secret as it was meant to be.

But the incident with the chapati unnerved me like nothing else had. I have witnessed Swamiji's powers time and again, but to experience it at the same time in both the mystical and mundane aspects of life was rather unsettling.

I remember many years ago, I had a sandwich wager with Him. All my life, I've pretty much done as I pleased, so it wasn't easy to follow instructions at first. Swamiji had an important meeting scheduled around lunchtime. It was decided that we'll give Him a sandwich before the meeting and one after. Swamiji asked me to make the sandwich fresh after He'd pressed the kitchen buzzer. Vidya Swami had been up early and had to recite the Lalita Sahasranama in the evening so I asked him to rest, and I'd clean up after and leave. There were just fifteen more minutes before the clock would hit 1.30 pm, and I figured Swamiji's hour-long meeting would be coming to an end.

I quickly cut the corners of four slices of bread (though He cuts no corners in His life, He likes the bread's corners cut), buttered them, placed a cheese slice, a layer of cheese-mushroom mix, and thin tomato slices. It was all ready; I now simply had to toast it on the hotplate when the buzzer rang. It'd save time, I thought. I once read a quote by Bill Gates that fits me to the T.

'I choose a lazy person to do a hard job. Because a lazy person will find an easy way to do it.'

I was just that lazy person. Making sandwiches hardly qualified as a tough job; it was just my principle in life, to get things done in a swift manner. Lingering over anything wasn't something I enjoyed, except delicious chocolate desserts. The buzzer rang some twenty minutes later. I had kept the hotplate heated and ready, so the sandwich was nice and toasty in seconds. Swamiji was drinking water, seemed a bit exhausted from all the speaking but His usual cheerful self.

I set the plate down and the knife and the fork. He always eats with a knife and a fork, all that can be eaten with a knife and a fork. The idea of food on His fingers is intolerable to Him. It's endearing to see Him quickly rise from the dining table to wash hands if there's even a smear of gravy or spices on His hands. It's a rare occurrence anyway.

Going back to the sandwich story, as soon as He put a morsel of the sandwich in His mouth, He said, 'You made it earlier, this sandwich?'

'Swamiji, it's freshly grilled.'

'No, it isn't, Bhikkuram, you made the sandwich a while back.'

I smiled sheepishly, 'Just the filling and then I covered it nicely. And grilled it fresh for you.'

'I specifically asked you to make everything fresh,' He gave me a stern look.

'It's almost fresh, Swamiji, and how do you even know that it's not,' I said in consternation.

'When you prepared the bread in advance, it lost its moisture, so it's a bit dry at the edges and soft at the center. It's not because of the heat but being kept out in the open. Hence, the change in taste.'

I refused to believe that preparing a sandwich a few minutes early had altered its taste to such a degree. I said to Swamiji that

I'd go back in the kitchen and make a fresh sandwich, grill just like this one (I had another ready-to-eat sandwich waiting on the kitchen slab) and then place them side by side, and He wouldn't be able to tell the difference. If I win, then I get to revel in my triumph, and if He wins, then not only will I humbly apologize but listen to Him in all kitchen matters. Swamiji agreed to the wager, 'Sure, bring it on.'

I went back and made the fresh sandwich exactly the same as the spare one. Next, I grilled them both side by side. The end result was that they both looked the same, in presentation, quality, and texture. I was so certain that Swamiji would bite into each one and not be able to tell the old from the new.

I was so thrilled that for once I was about to get the better of Him that I walked into His study with a smug smile on my face.

'Swamiji, here are the sandwiches, bon appétit.'

Even before I had set the tray down, He pointed to the sandwich on the right and said, 'That's the old one, and this is the fresh one.'

I was stunned. How could He tell? He hadn't even taken a bite yet.

'But you haven't even tasted them,' sulkily I served Him the fresh sandwich.

'I don't need to.'

Flexing His knuckles, grinning mischievously, He had leaned back in the chair and said, 'Even if you were to make orange juice out of say six oranges, and one of them was rotten, I could pinpoint the particular orange and the order in which it had been added to the juicer.'

Never again did I disregard Swamiji's instructions and carried them out as it is. I've always been a bit of a health freak and had this silly notion that I knew food well. Every time I tried to offer my unsolicited two cents to Swamiji regarding His meals or rest, He'd say to me, 'Bhikkuram, you forget, I am the author of *The Wellness Sense* and not you.'

There was no matching Swamiji's humor. His words, forever laced with love and kindness, endeared Him to everyone repeatedly. He would diffuse the grimmest situations with such charm and wit that you had no choice but to bow to His superior intelligence.

Despite Swamiji's preference for His food a certain way, my own style seeped into my preparations. I had very little experience in the kitchen before I came to the ashram. I could spend hours writing poetry in the garden, but ask me to step in the kitchen and I'd break into a sweat. Sadhvi Shraddha had little experience like myself, as she was in the corporate sector for many years before she shifted to the ashram. When, during Swamiji's solitude in 2017, we bonded over our meals, I realized that for both of us the kitchen was a relatively new domain. We were both in the same rocky boat. It made us really nervous to cook for our Guru.

One morning, I prayed to Sri Hari to bless us both with good culinary skills. For it didn't matter who cooked the meal, the only thing that mattered was that it nourished Swamiji's delicate health. It's difficult to feed Him anything that isn't made well.

It was one of the most peaceful moments in my heart when Swamiji had said to me, 'You know, Bhikkuram, what's so unique about your food?' I shook my head.

'It's delicious and so light afterward. I'm hungry again in a couple of hours, which is the mark of a good meal.'

In fact, He asked me once how it is that even the pasta, baked and cheesy dishes I made tasted so light. It didn't aggravate His breathing or trigger asthma, as it normally did sometimes.

'I never use any heavy cream, butter, and rarely ever use olive oil, Swamiji.

'What are you cooking it in then?'

'*Sarson ke tel*, mustard oil, and fresh white butter,' I said with a wide grin on my face.

Swamiji laughed heartily, it was inconceivable to Him that I had been feeding Him pasta, His most favorite cuisine, cooked in our *desi* mustard oil. He, who had dined in the finest restaurants in the world, was highly amused. It tickled Him that the Italian, Mexican, and continental cooking was all happening in what Vidya Swami (being a South Indian) called, '*Garibon ka tel*, poor man's oil.'

Well, the poor man's oil suited Swamiji's health and mine a lot. I had grown up eating this oil, as on mamma's side in the cold regions of Jammu and Kashmir, this is the oil they used. In mustard oil's defense, it might not have had the Mediterranean ancestry of olive oil, but it had zero carbs and hence its glycemic index was zero too. I continued to experiment with His meals and often tried to apply my writing techniques when coming up with recipes in the kitchen.

When they come out right, Swamiji's praise is evident in the way His face lights up when He takes a look at the dish. It takes Him just one glance to tell Vidya Swami and me if the food is done right, whether salt, chili, or anything else is needed. It has never happened that Swamiji does not eat the food we make, maybe just leave a little if it's not too great, but He has never broken our heart or confidence by saying the food isn't good even when it isn't. His kindness is beyond me.

That and also the fact that tears start rolling down my cheeks fast if I detect even the slightest sign on His face that the food isn't to His liking. He often says to Vidya Swami, 'Just eat it quietly because if she starts crying then we'll be here forever.'

There's a pampering, a babying in His manner to those in His service. He treats each one like a child, knowing well that His approval as a parent means everything to them. Vidya Swami is such a giant but even he's like a toddler around Swamiji, saying Bauji Bauji, all the time.

When Vidya Swami's mother passed away in 2018, he acted as if everything was fine. I've always seen him so detached that I figured he meant it when he said, 'Everyone has to go, it was her time.'

Swamiji was abroad at that time. On his return, when Vidya Swami was finally alone with his Guru, he broke down like a two-year-old. I couldn't imagine the strong and nonchalant Vidya Swami breaking down like that, but he cried like a baby. All of us are like that in front of Him, no more than little children looking up at Him to fix life's small and big problems for us.

Once, when Vidya Swami sought Swamiji's blessing for his mother's surgery, He immediately transferred a couple of lacs to his account. He did the same for the next surgery and for Vidya Swami's younger brother's marriage the year after. Money to Swamiji has always been a commodity meant to be given away. No matter what His current financial state may have been, His hand is always stretched to give.

Sunny, my brother, had been working on some wireframes and UI designs for one of Swamiji's projects. He wasn't expecting any remuneration at all but when he was paid several thousand euros, I had to say, 'Swamiji, why did we pay him so much, it's a lot of money and there's so much outflow happening with your other projects. It was so unnecessary, Swamiji, Sunny was just happy to do it as a seva.'

'Bhikkuram, you know that's not my working style to take seva. If someone has delivered, then they must be paid. Besides, I know it'll come handy to him.'

I didn't make much of it until a month later on a call, my brother said that it was so kind of Swamiji to give him a big bonus. He had really needed it just then, as he had just taken out a big mortgage. It's always so uncanny that Swamiji knows exactly what's going on in the lives of the people who are associated with Him in any way. It's actually a new normal where we know that He knows what's going on in the lives, hearts, and minds of His disciples, devotees, and if need be, of a random stranger.

Kind Are His Ways

We were in Delhi before flying out for the Kundalini camp in Pune. A few months earlier, my ex-in-laws from my previous life tracked me down to my new life. They were keen on returning a piece of gold jewelry that belonged to me once. At the time of the divorce, it seemed they had misplaced it somewhere. Now many years later, it bothered my ex-mother-in-law that it was still with her.

Life has a way of making most people see things in a different light with the passage of time. They came down to Chandigarh to return it to me. It was an emotional moment because I had known them since my teens, and it was nostalgic to see them, especially because they were the same age as my parents, who were gone now. The couple seemed older, vulnerable, and worried about their son, as is always the case with parents as they age.

They knew a bit about Swamiji, and I told them some more. They expressed a desire to meet Him, and I said I'll see if it's possible when we are in Delhi next. When I asked Swamiji, He happily agreed to grant them five minutes for a personal meeting.

A few months later, we were in Delhi, and they came to have Swamiji's darshan. They sat mesmerized as Swamiji asked after them. His beautiful heart and countenance totally blew them away. Swamiji's magnetism is powered by His truthful speech. He can disarm anyone by shining the light of His words on their hopeless faces. He can charm the birds out of the woods, fish out of water, grief out of hearts, and death out of ailing bodies. Soon, my ex mother-in-law opened up and said to Swamiji that she longed for a grandchild. Both her children had no such inclination. She sounded tired and worried about what the future held. Finally, she asked for His help.

Swamiji's eyes, as He sat there on a long sofa in His fiery ochre robe, were so filled with compassion as He heard her plea. Once in a while, He'd give me a reassuring glance that all was well. I'm always a bit tense if anyone whom I've known meets Him. I fear that they'd inadvertently say something disrespectful to my Guru out of ignorance, and I'd not be able to stand it and lash out at them.

One mustn't treat a Guru as one's friends or just another person they are seeking advice from. There's a certain way of addressing them and being in their presence; love is one thing, reverence another. After Swamiji patiently heard them out, He said, 'You must respect your children's decision.'

When she persisted, He said gravely, 'I could tell you the reason for it, but it'd be a breach of their privacy. And I can't do that.'

The moment He said that, I knew He had hit a nerve. The in-laws already knew what the issue was, but they didn't expect Swamiji to know it. He sent them with His blessings and thanked them for looking after me for the time I was with them. It melted my heart to hear Swamiji say that. I doubt that even my own family could have cared for me as He did, making good on every promise simply because of the one He had given to my mother.

It's His eternal kindness that fills me with such deep gratitude that I sometimes really don't know what to do with it. I try to pour it into poems, books, and my spirit of service, but it falls short of His noble stature in every way, as it was with the previous drafts of this book.

In Him I Trust

I love pestering Bhagavān and the Divine Mother with my fervent praying. I'm certain that Sri Hari hears my prayers.

These two lines that Swamiji had added to tweak my author bio did what a decade of my struggles couldn't do – make me feel secure in Sri Hari's love. I knew Bhagavān and Maa loved me, as it's their thing to love everyone, but I also had begun to believe that somewhere inside the beautiful silent and dark *vigraha* was a being who found me endearing, just as I did them. I have always shied away a lot from allowing myself to feel such things, firstly because Swamiji has always been insistent about cultivating humility in oneself. I particularly lack this trait, so it literally burns my ears to even think of myself as a devotee of the beautiful Lord.

But as time has gone by, I've come to know this intriguing thing about me, I can't stay away from Sri Hari's *vigraha* for long. It has always held a magnetic power over me, more so now. If the sanctum-sanctorum is open, then you'll find me there. As I planned to write this book, I had grand plans to sit on my desk and finish writing. On the first day itself Sri Hari told me to get my stuff and do my writing next to them in the temple. But I just wasn't in the mood of carrying everything back to the temple at 9 am everyday especially, when I had already been there for a few hours, dressing them and then doing my morning japa. But when God commands every blade of grass moves, and so did I.

As is my nature to say no to everything when I hear it for the first time, I said to them, 'What? Get all my stuff, all the paraphernalia – Laptop, iPad, notebook and breakfast?' I double-checked. 'All of it?'

Bhagavān smiling that sideways smile that's trademark Sri Hari, spoke it loud and clear in my head, 'Yes, all of it.'

Maybe it's hard for some to imagine that such a conversation is possible, between a living person and a stone idol. But it is not as impossible as one might think. From being absolute strangers to parents to every other relationship on the human spectrum, Sri Hari has filled all roles for me. He is whomever you wish Him to be. The only catch is that it takes time, a lot of time. And since time was all I had, it's what I offered to the *vigraha*, that and lots of salty tears and drama. Not sure though, if the last one worked in my favor.

My efforts would have all been in vain if it weren't for Swamiji's powerful blessings. There are enough people I know who've been praying to Bhagavān all their lives, and with all sorts of rituals and fanfare, and yet Sri Hari has not shown up as He and Maa do sometimes in my japa. It was during the course of an ordinary conversation that Swamiji had said to a handful of His disciples, 'There are only two people in the world Sri

Hari has asked me to look after: one is Raghu Swami and the other is Bhikkuram.'

It only strengthened my resolve to be more in Sri Hari's line of sight as they were in mine. All of it was impossible though, without the force of Swamiji's grace. He was the string that held the pearls together.

Just like a terrified child or an abandoned pup places her paw in the new master's hands, sensing she's safe, placing one's trust in Swamiji was being rescued from the vicious world. I had accepted this a while back that if anyone could take me closer to Bhagavān, it was Him. This sentence may not be grammatically sound, but as time went by, this truth kept staring me in the face that He was Him. He was the savior indeed.

On a winter evening, outside of Swamiji's meeting room, devotees sat waiting for their personal meeting. A young woman, anxious and panicking, was creating a scene to see Swamiji. It was already 8:30 pm, and Swamiji had been speaking for the last two hours. It had been a long day already. When the commotion outside reached Swamiji's ears, He summoned Vidu Swami, His aide, to find out what the matter was.

Seconds later, Swamiji marched out, walking past a circle of devotees to speak to the young woman. His gentle demeanor and the kindness with which He spoke calmed her down in seconds.

Five minutes later, everything went back to normal, and while walking back to the cottage, Swamiji said to Vidu Swami, 'I might have left from the back door if everything was well, but when things are not okay, Om Swami never takes the escape route.'

'Sorry, Guru Maharaj, I was only thinking of you, your convenience.'

'I appreciate that. But when everyone deserts someone, that is the time you'll always find me present. They've placed their trust in me. I'm the only shield they have. The question of leaving from the back door doesn't arise.'

I've always known this to be true. He never leaves when you are in trouble, not even when all you have is a *potli*, a bundle, of sorrow and afflictions. I should know; it's all I had when I first met Swamiji a decade ago. Having His darshan was the biggest turning point in my sorry life. Swamiji was the miracle I had long been waiting for.

Sujata Om Aurora, an amazing human being, a dedicated ashram trustee, and unwavering devotee of Swamiji, and I were once traveling in her car. She has this beautiful, sweet, husky voice and has impeccable command over English and Hindi. Funnily enough, whenever she says, 'Sadhviji' in her pure Hindi, to my ears, it sounds like 'Netaji,' as if I'm a politician being asked to comment on matters of national importance. It is really quite endearing. Anyway, I digress.

So, during the course of the three-hour long ride, we spoke of many things. One of the things that stayed with me was, 'Sadhviji, everyone keeps saying they've seen these incredible miracles in their life by Swamiji's grace. I wish I also have an experience like that someday.' Out of nowhere, a pang of unease had sprung in my heart.

'Sujata, you don't want that. To experience His grace means there's something gravely wrong in one's life. Ask me, I've seen plenty... miracles.'

Hellfire

It was soon to be New Year's Eve. The hustle-bustle at the ashram was in full swing. Swamiji's meeting schedule was packed with personal and group meetings, both in the morning and evening. He'd come up sometimes as early as 9 am to attend His meetings. It was around the time that my japa in the temple got over too. Sometimes, I'd head straight to seek His blessings in the meeting room. Some days, I just knew that I must go see Swamiji now. It was a sixth sense that I had been summoned by my Guru.

Also, by Sri Hari's grace, I started to have some proficiency in assessing the expressions on their faces. Just as a child knows upon seeing the face of her mother or father whether they are happy, sad, upset, or unwell, I too had developed an awareness of Sri Hari. Their proximity, simplicity, and love being the most beautiful and sacred aspect of my life, how could I then not know if something was amiss or not.

On that bright winter morning, the garden was full of devotees as they waited their turn to meet Swamiji. I met a few, avoided a few, as sometimes conversations can be long, and in the mornings, there was always much to do.

I requested Vidu Swamiji to allow me in as soon as Swamiji's current meeting was over. Minutes later, I was offering my pranams to Swamiji. He sat on His *asana* like a great yogi, His presence towering the room. Anyone who went into the meeting room invariably agreed that Swamiji's presence dwarfed everything around them. He seemed so tall and vast like the sky. For even though He was seated, it felt like His height and width had doubled.

The sun rays from His divinity lit up the room more than the light bulb. He looked very much like the awesome Lord Vishnu I've believed Him to be since my darshan of Him in His Vaman avatara and my mother's vision in Vaikuntha.

It has always felt to me that His power is most apparent when He sits on His *asana*, whether in the temple or in the meeting room, for He sits there to give, resolve, absolve people of their sorrows. Today when I entered, Swamiji mentioned that there was a bushfire raging in Australia. The homes of His neighbors on two sides had been razed to the ground. The fire was turning everything into ashes. About Swamiji's countryside residence and the neighbors behind Him, the lovely Catherine and Brian's home, there was no news yet.

'Rescue missions are slow because whole towns are burning.'

'Swamiji, you know everything, please just see with your divine sight if the house is still there.'

A faint smile appeared on His lips, 'You know well, Bhikkuram, that I'll do no such thing. It'll be what it has to be.'"

I tried to gather my feelings to empathize, but try as I might, in my heart I could neither find the right words nor sad feelings. I experienced no sorrow at all and instead felt quite upbeat.

'Swamiji, nothing has happened to the house. I just don't feel …everything is fine, else Bhagavān would have told me.'

'Bhikkuram, go read the news when you get back to your room. Thousands of people have lost their homes. The fire is still raging and there's blinding and suffocating smoke and soot everywhere...so we don't really know.'

It was my turn that day to serve the evening supper with Vidya Swami, and the situation was still the same with the bushfires. It seemed like New Year's Eve was going to be a sad affair. Swamiji was due to give a discourse in half an hour, and what was supposed to be a beautiful, joyful evening was, in my head, consumed by this bushfire.

Swamiji saw my melancholy, and His face immediately softened. 'We don't have any news yet; let's wait until tomorrow.'

I just sat there upset, with the world, and Swamiji for not stopping it from happening. For He saved other people why couldn't He save His own home. What was the big deal? When I continued to stay silent, a hint of a smile appeared on Swamiji's face.

'Bhikkuram, you were quite perceptive in the morning… we'll be okay.'

My eyes lit up, 'What does okay mean?'

'They'll write in tomorrow to say the house is all good.'

'I knew it! But why wouldn't you tell me, Swamiji?' I was astonished at the solemn look Swamiji had maintained throughout the day.

'Because you can't keep anything to yourself,' He had smiled.

Sure enough the next day Swamiji received news from Catherine and Brian, that the only houses standing in that vicinity were theirs and Swamiji's.

Everything else around them was burnt to the ground.

I wasn't surprised, as Catherine, a lovely lady in her sixties, would often bake fresh bread and also often leave vegan meals at His doorstep. It came as no surprise to me that their house was fine. Swamiji never forgot anyone who had ever offered Him even a morsel. The elderly couple had His protection; He had saved them.

When the next day the pictures came in, they were simply mind-boggling. The fire had reached Swamiji's front door and was barely a few feet away. Looking at the pictures, it appeared as if the flames, the Fire God, had prostrated before Swamiji's porch, offering his salutation and had retreated from there.

What's even more baffling is that, less than ten yards from Swamiji's front door, was an entire row of tall bamboo shoots. The bamboo should have caught the flames, a flying spark, but it didn't. Had that happened, absolutely nothing of the house would have remained. There was a large wooden deck that could have easily caught fire. The flames that had swallowed miles and miles of forests, townships, and cattle had turned away from Swamiji's front door, even when the tall, dried bamboo was just the stuff it needed to burn the house in a matter of minutes. When I had read the bushfire news online, it had momentarily paralyzed my senses.

> *Batemans Bay and surrounding areas, on the NSW South Coast, were hit by the terrifying Currowan fire, described as a '500,000-hectare inferno'. The fire burnt for 74 days, after starting from a lightning strike on November 26, 2019, and has gone on well into the New year. Thousands are homeless and stranded on beaches with their children and pets. The fire has claimed countless lives both human and wild animals. Brave firefighters have lost their lives to the raging furnace. With each passing day the rescue missions have become harder as the flames tall as the sky are swallowing everything in its path.*

Catherine's email a couple of days later said that if only there was rain, the fire would start to die down. There was simply no relief from the blazing inferno. Swamiji was just finishing replying to her when I asked, 'So, will you send the rain there?'

He looked up from His laptop and just smiled.

The next day, Catherine wrote in saying that most unexpectedly it rained in that region and it calmed the fire down. People had been hoping for rain for weeks and it hadn't happened. And within thirty-six hours of Swamiji's assurance that it would rain, it poured.

I smiled when I saw the news online of it raining in Batemans Bay, thinking, 'Well, here goes the Rainmaker again.'

Something that has always surprised me is that for His devotee, Swamiji can and will do what's necessary but for Himself He wouldn't lift a finger, leaving it to Mother Divine to do as She sees fit.

matkarmakṛnmatparamomadbhaktaḥ saṅgavarjitaḥ |
nirvairaḥ sarvabhūteṣuyaḥ sa māmeti pāṇḍava ||

O' Pandava! Whoever works for Me, looks upon Me as the Supreme, is devoted to Me, is free from all kinds of attachment and has no enmity towards all living beings, such a person comes directly to Me.

Bhagavad Gita, 11.55.

2020

Don't Tell

The Jaipur Literature Fest in the pink city every year is a grand affair. Swamiji was invited to speak about His book, *The Book of Kindness*. The Astrology Camp in Delhi had just wrapped up, and we flew down to Jaipur. It was a crazy turnout as people lined up to get books signed by Him, especially after they had heard Him speak. On a winter morning in January, Swamiji in His black robe dazzled on the stage like a tall mountain, radiating His usual gentle strength and stillness. His perspective on life, on God, and political issues were appreciated by the audience with thunderous applause.

It always makes Swamiji shy to be the recipient of such attention, whether in the ashram or any public forum. His innate nature is to be *ekaki*, to be alone. Six months in a year, He sets aside to recover from all the interactions, recharge Himself, so He can be there for us. India being His most taxing stint in terms of daily interactions and personal meetings. It's draining for someone like Him who prefers to work quietly. Think of one of those silent and brilliant children in the classroom who loves to sit in a corner and work on difficult math calculations. That'd be Him in a different life.

After the successful event at the Lit Fest, we stayed on in Jaipur for three more days. Many devotees came down to see and hear Swamiji at the Lit Fest. On one of the days while we were in Jaipur, a loving family sent in Swamiji's lunch. There were many elaborate preparations and an insane amount of food to choose from. Vidya Swami and I served Swamiji a little bit of everything. Mid-way through the meal, Swamiji asked us if everyone was feeling alright.

We felt great, who wouldn't, seeing such yummy home-cooked food. Vidya Swami and I ate carefully, leaving some dishes aside, as we wanted to save space for the tempting home-made chocolate brownies by a loving devotee.

Some minutes later, Swamiji said that His vision was a bit hazy. He then asked Vidu Swami to stand at a distance. Swamiji left His food in between and with His palm covering one eye, gazed at Vidu Swami. In a matter-of-fact voice, He said to him, 'I can only see one side of your face.'

It made no sense to the three of us, was He serious or teasing, sometimes He does that. Next moment Swamiji rushed us out, saying, 'I think I need to lie down. I'm just exhausted.'

We weren't surprised because there's always some allergy in His eyes. Since Swamiji is forever overworked, there's never really any time to recover properly from these frequent irritations either. In the evening, we were supposed to go out for dinner. Swamiji told us that we would leave as planned. Vidya Swami packed the food back in the hot cases and tucked the dish carrying brownies under his arm.

Some four hours later, when we knocked at Swamiji's door, we were aghast to see that He looked pale and unwell. His eyes were red and swollen, and He was still resting up. This was so unlike Him.

'What's wrong, Swamiji?' I felt a sudden fear in the pit of my stomach.

Swamiji spoke slowly, 'Uh well…I had lost complete vision in my right eye. It's back now, a bit blurry, but I can see.'

'Swamiji…' I could barely string two words together. My brain felt like it was frozen, and Vidya Swami stood rooted like a teddy bear with a stunned expression. It was Vidu Swami who broke that spell. 'Swamiji, you've to see a doctor.'

'I think I'll wait… I think I had food poisoning or an allergic reaction of some sort.'

Vidya Swami was quick to say that it could have been one of the local delicacies, 'Must be the Aloe Vera dish, Bauji.'

Vidya Swami and I hadn't tasted that preparation, and Vidu Swami had barely touched it. Maybe it's why none of us were affected.

'You could be right, Motu. I had difficulty breathing too, and then it triggered an asthma attack. There was no cold milk in the fridge.'

'Oh Swamiji, why didn't you call us?'

He had been in agony for hours, lying there unable to breathe, see, but He didn't call us. Swamiji does not drink milk, but during an asthma attack, the cold milk usually helps. We would have arranged it from the reception had He just called us. I was both angry at Him for not calling us and frightened that something terrible could have happened to Him while we were next door eating brownies. I felt all shaky inside and just wanted to have a good cry.

Seeing our anxious and worried faces, He let out a laugh. It relaxed us a little, and then Swamiji immediately said, 'Now who wants dinner?'

It's the most endearing thing about Swamiji; He always diffuses even the tensest situations by dismissing it as if it was nothing.

Swamiji asked us to give Him ten minutes to get ready, and just then, muttering something to himself, Vidu Swami got up to leave. Swamiji stopped Him immediately.

'Now don't you tell the devotees, especially the family who sent the meal. I'm fine now. This will really upset them; all's well now.'

And so, not a word was uttered about the scare we had to anyone. Even when all the devotees gathered on the last evening in His suite to have His darshan, He met them as if nothing had happened, even though He was still recovering from the severe reaction. His care for the well-being of people exceeds logic. So many times, I just can't relate to Swamiji. More than a hundred times I've seen Him ready for a string of meetings or go up for a discourse in the temple, mostly both, one after the other, when He's in no state to do so.

Whenever I say to Him, 'Please just cancel for once.' That it's alright; everyone loves Him, and they'll understand that He's unwell. He replies, 'I know they won't mind; their love for me is immense, but my love for them is even greater. Many of them have come from so far, spending resources, time, and money they don't have. I can't not go see them.'

The Fallen Leaf

Barely two weeks after the Jaipur incident, in the first week of February, came the news that Brahmachari Rishi, an initiate in the white vastra, had slipped down the hill of his tiny hut. Rishi was in his mid-twenties and armed with a master's in physics. Swamiji clearly loved him and fondly addressed him as Buah. Rishi's late father used to call him by this nickname.

This young initiate shared a unique bond with his Guru. I remember dining with him in Bangalore for the first time when we had gone for the launch of *A Million Thoughts*. Swamiji was pleasantly surprised to see Rishi at the venue and dragged him back with us to the hotel.

Soon, thereafter, Brahmachari Rishi came to live in the ashram. Once I got to know him, he became like a younger brother to me. He was from Kolkata and had a superb sense of humor. I'd often tease him by calling him the Bengal Tiger. The demise of his father had deeply affected him, and he looked upon

Swamiji, not merely as his Guru, but as his father. There was a quiet and vulnerable child inside of him and that's what Swamiji saw every time He looked at him.

In fact, Swamiji attended a Spiritual Confluence of world leaders in Kolkata many years ago. In the early days, He travelled alone and on this particular trip, as He gave His speech on that huge open forum, in scorching heat and humidity, He was badly sunburnt. Having been in the Himalayas for so long during His sadhana, He was no longer used to being exposed to the sun. As Swamiji finished His speech and was getting off the dais, it was Rishi who showed up holding a big black umbrella. He held it over Swamiji's head and on the verge of tears, he had said to Swamiji, 'Why is there no one with you? You shouldn't travel alone, Swamiji.'

On more than two occasions, I've heard Swamiji reminisce about this incident. This bright and intelligent young man who captured Swamiji's heart, had a great future ahead of him. Swamiji was keen to train him, so that he could accompany Him in His travels in due course. But it was not to be.

Finally, tangible news from the hospital came that Rishi's spinal cord was badly injured. The disbelief everyone experienced was phenomenal because he was moving about the ashram just fine, and the next day this catastrophe had happened. As a couple of days passed, it started to become clearer that he wasn't going to be walking anytime soon. There was a long road of recovery ahead. It was heartbreaking to see him in the hospital; the spine and ribs had broken, but his tangerine humor was intact.

I tried to offer him soup, placing a spoon in his mouth, but my hands shook. I could feel the sting of tears. I had some very happy memories with him. He looked like a child of no more than twelve or fourteen as he lay in the ICU. He was in a lot of pain, but that didn't stop him from smiling and reassuring me not to cry for him. I wished there was a way to turn back the clock. I was sure that if there was a way, Swamiji would do it for Brahmachari Rishi in a heartbeat.

After the initial shock wave that hit the ashram settled, the administration tried to figure out how Rishi slipped from that otherwise very safe space. He had fallen early in the morning and must have been lying there in the cold for at least four hours before he was discovered. The news had spread like wildfire in the nearby village.

The police paid a visit as well, making enquiries and inspecting the area where it had all transpired. Swamiji wasn't in the ashram when this incident took place. On His return, the recent developments were reported to Swamiji by the trust. Their perplexity over how Rishi ended up there was a major cause of concern.

Swamiji cleared all the confusion in a matter of seconds.

'As much as it saddens me to share this, the truth is Brahmachari Rishi didn't fall or slip, he actually jumped.'

There was such lingering sadness on Swamiji's face as He said, 'I know this to be the truth because Mother Earth told me herself. The hill he jumped from is not at a great height. Rishi ran barefoot for at least a few hundred yards, to gain momentum right before he jumped. The thick water pipe running below halted his fall else his head would have hit a rock. It'd have been fatal. Sri Hari saved him.'

The dutiful Maa Shamata, Swamiji's most dedicated disciple, was with Rishi from the moment she heard about his condition. Things were progressing slowly as there were many complications since the spinal cord had snapped into two.

Despite the diagnosis, everyone was hopeful that with Swamiji's blessings, Rishi would start walking in due course.

Later in the week, Swamiji received an update from Maa Shamata on Rishi's reports. Vidya Swami was just as fond of Rishi as I. We both loved to treat Rishi to healthy fast food from our kitchen, as his cottage was right next door.

Swamiji stayed non-communicative, and I timidly asked him, 'Is Brahmachari Rishi doing alright, Swamiji?' The sad look in His eyes deepened as He said, 'It was such a foolish thing to do, had he only waited for my return.' Without saying anything more, Swamiji turned on Chopin's Nocturnes that made the air melancholier.

Foolish as it was, I understood to some degree why Rishi had gone up there. It could easily have been me. There's something so fragile about one's mental balance that when it tips, no matter how hard you try to hold onto your sanity you just can't get a grip on it.

I now also understood why whenever I pleaded with Swamiji that I didn't want to live He'd dismiss it saying it's not going to happen. When I made self-deprecating jokes about how I should just jump from a hill or a tall building, He'd laugh at first and then sternly say, 'Just remember, if you jump you won't die but it's possible that you'd be in no state to do anything else for the rest of your life.'

I'd come up with newer ideas all the time.

'What if the leopard that was spotted near the ashram takes me.'

'Well, you still are not going to die, it'll probably just take one arm and leave the rest of you,' Swamiji would make the whole thing hilarious in an instant. It's why in His company, it feels so safe.

All the weaknesses in my head just sat mesmerized. In that moment there was no insanity, only a deep desire to be well, to live, to hear Him speak and learn from Him how to lead a life which was of use to the world.

Every month, at least once or twice, greatly distressed by my mental state, I'd contemplate ways to end my life. And it's the pure truth that it was only His warning that any stupid choice I made wasn't going to let me die on His watch. But being unable to do anything else and vegetate for the rest of my life saved me every time from making an irrevocable mistake. I believed His every word. So, when Rishi's news came, the first thing that occurred to me was that Swamiji not only saved Rishi, He saved me too.

That evening as He sat there quietly listening to Beethoven, I waited for the piece to get over.

'Swamiji, I know you are sad because of Rishi, but with your blessings, he'll be well again.' A shadow of a smile passed His face.

'Bhikkuram, you give me too much credit, attribute too many things to me, when the truth is that I'm merely a medium of the Divine Mother's will.'

'Swamiji, you are the Divine Mother…you'll do something for Rishi, I know.'

'A leaf once broken from a tree can't be joined, no matter how hard it wishes…the damage to the spinal cord is extreme, it can't just be reversed, not yet.'

Under Swamiji's directions, the ashram took care of Rishi's hospital expenses. Some generous devotees also came forth, and finally, Rishi was shifted to Kolkata, his hometown, to be in his mother's care. In the years that followed, Swamiji encouraged him to learn programming so he could be financially independent and, more than that, use his beautiful and intelligent mind to greater use.

The truth is just one wrong turn can change the entire course of our lives; from some places, there's no turning back. We can set things right, make amends, but like the broken leaf from a tree, some things just can't be joined back. Beware of those choices, seek help, and you'll find that it's possible to heal completely. To be embarrassed about being mentally unwell is one of the worst things we can do to ourselves. The good, bad, and ugly, whatever it is, it's a part of us and it deserves our attention. And for every mentally unbalanced person, there's at least one strong person around who can prod them on the road to recovery. All that's wrong and all that's right with us, our flaws, virtues, they are all housed under one roof. We are home to a beautiful person, and the same person can at times be unwell. That's all there is to it. To quote Swamiji here:

'Happiness is also an art, and it can be learned.'

On a lighter note, I'm reminded of this particular anecdote. Once someone from the audience had asked Swamiji to tell something about the secret project (Sadhana App was under wraps at that time) He was working on for Sanatana Dharma. His head tilted to the side, and with an utmost serious expression on His face, Swamiji had replied, 'I'd tell you but then I'd have to kill you.'

Samsara to Sannyasa

A while back, during an event, a sharp and witty young man had a confession to make. I admired his nerve, for most people shy away from making such admissions. I thought him to be very brave, as it's not everyone's cuppa to be truthful about things that don't always show one in a flattering light. It both tickled me and made me think how one can never really escape the snares of Samsara. It's like the more you try to outrun it, the faster it starts to chase you. But can it really give chase when you are happy to turn back and face it?

So, let's turn back. When I was compiling anecdotes from my life for the book, I asked him if he was okay sharing his confession with the world. Without a moment's hesitation, he was onboard. In Tejas Om Gupta's own words, here's an account of how sometimes what we see is not exactly how things are.

My Impression of Sadhvi Vrinda Om Before her Initiation

Like many of us, it was Swamiji's book If Truth Be Told *through which I got to know about Swamiji. The book was launched in December of 2014, and I got my hands on it in January of 2015. The desire to meet and see Swamiji took place, and it materialized in October of 2015 when the first Ashram meditation camp happened.*

By this time, I devoured all the information there was online related to Swamiji or the people close to Him, so when I went to Ashram for the first time I was just putting names on people's faces I had seen in pictures online.

That was when I first time saw Sadhvi Vrinda ji who was then (Ismita), she was wearing a green saree and was manning the makeshift book stall which consisted of a chair and a table on which the books were kept. I noticed she was smiling to herself and had an excitement in her eyes, I recognized her. I went near the books and inquired about some of the books, and she told me most jubilantly and that was it.

I again briefly saw her at a children's retreat at Neemrana, where I had a brief interaction with her over the buffet. She had made a funny remark about the food, and we just laughed. After this I started frequenting Ashram quite often, but I never had any exchange with Sadhviji, but many people would talk about her, some devotees who had exchanges with her in the past or had spent some time with her told me that she can be extremely rude at times and somewhat mercurial, some people found her dismissive and inconsiderate.

Although I had no such personal experience with her, my mind was probably getting subtly conditioned about her, but I didn't give it much thought.

Then someone told me about an incident that happened in Ashram and probably because of Sadhviji, a village boy was sent to jail. When I heard this story, it seemed unjust and unfair.

So, all these stories and narratives of Sadhviji were painted in my mind in addition to one beautiful thing that she would always laud someone profusely if she liked something or something about someone.

Anyway, this was just bits and pieces of information which I had but since I was not connected with her or had any exchanges with her or seen her that much until her initiation day, I never gave it a second thought.

Somewhere in my mind there was an image of her that she is probably someone from whom I should stay away from.

Sadhviji's Initiation Day and How it Impacted Me

In July 2016, it was the first Guru Poornima event which was being celebrated where more than 100 devotees were present. It was my first time being in the Ashram on Guru Poornima. Some of us devotees were waiting for Swamiji to come near the old meeting room. Suddenly, I saw someone coming up towards the meeting room in ochre robes. It was not Swamiji, she was wearing a saree, an ochre saree and her hair was tied at the back in a kind of bun. I recognized the face, it was Sadhviji, she had just been initiated. I remember being surprised and exclaiming in Punjabi 'Aah Ki?' 'Oh, What's this!' I could see a sense of calmness on her face, she seemed content, she had a glow on her face.

Swamiji came for discourse in the morning, yes those were the times: everyone was ecstatic to be near Swamiji, in

His presence. Swamiji walked in His usual majestic and most graceful gait, He wore His black robe, it was divinity personified in front of us. After Swamiji paid His obeisance to Sri Hari Bhagavān in the Sanctum Sanctorum, He sat down on His asana and asked about our well-being, He does that unfailingly till date. I was sitting huddled right in front of Him.

Swamiji announced that He had initiated Sadhvi Vrinda ji into Sanayasa who was formerly Ismita Tandon and from then everyone is to address her as Sadhviji, Sadhvi Vrinda or SV in short. Then Swamiji said something really powerful, 'No matter what anybody says, I know what is in her heart', Swamiji went on to say that He never for a moment forgets that she has no parents and Swamiji is all she has, Swamiji raised His hand and proclaimed that whatever blessing she will give to anyone it will come to pass.

Hearing Swamiji say these things about her just broke me down, I was in tears, tears of guilt, I felt guilty that somewhere I thought maybe she was not a good person and believed what people told me, I wept sitting in front of the temple while Swamiji was there.

Swamiji's words instilled a faith in me towards Sadhviji and a sense of respect and warmth.

Later I saw her going somewhere and I congratulated her, I was feeling happy for her and feeling the warmth in heart for her, which was effortless. Swamiji's words shifted something inside me.

Our Changed Equation in the Coming Years

The first thing which bewildered me was that soon after Sadhviji's initiation maybe a month or two later, I had her dream, it was surprising for me because I have had dreams of Swamiji, but I never expected a Swamiji's disciple to be in my dream. I was not expecting that at all. Later, when I met Sadhviji, I mentioned this to her, and she just smiled and nodded and said, maybe she and I will have some work to do together in the future.

I was living in Chandigarh then, and Sadhviji was living in Zirakpur, which is an adjoining city to Chandigarh. People would invite Sadhviji for satsang at their homes, and there, whenever she would narrate some story or share nuggets of wisdom, they would really make one think and fill one with hope. When she sang glories of Bhagavān, one could feel the bhaav. This was all very exciting for me; I would try my best to not miss a satsang. This increased my reverence for Sadhviji even more. I noticed that she was rather intuitive at certain things. Whenever she has told me something, I always believe it and never doubt it. What Swamiji said about her blessing someone will come to pass is permanently etched in my heart, and it also adds to my faith.

Over the years, I have found her to be very kind and gentle. One thing that stands out about her to me is that she does not hold back on giving credit, and if she has anything to give, she would happily do so.

Many times, when I would feel troubled or would feel stuck about a certain issue in my life, I would just shoot an email to her and she has never failed to respond. I have always felt better and hopeful, I am sure many can relate to this. She has silently helped me in humongous ways, which I got to know about later, and I am forever grateful to her.

I have seen her journey from the time of her initiation, I see how she has become carefree from what I have seen, the feeling of content is evident from her face. These days, when you are around her, you just feel better if you were not earlier, because around her, it is always a satsang. She silently prays for you, and from what I have seen, she has managed to get closer to Sri Hari than many of us. And Sri Hari never lets their devotees down. I know and believe that she is connected with Swamiji, Sri Hari, and whatever comes from her is coming from Them.

All Glories to Swamiji.

To simply appreciate Tejas's courage in sharing his thoughts is not enough. In the last ten years, I've seen how rare it is for people to appreciate others or acknowledge the help they've received. I'm reminded of the time when I was collecting stories for the *Book of Faith*. I knew someone who had been healed by Swamiji from severe depression that involved endangering one's own life and of her loved one. I thought it'd be a great addition to my anthology, as it'd give hope to people facing similar circumstances.

Excitedly, the lady shared her perspective in writing. It began with her first visit to the ashram and how pleasant it was. The wonderful hospitality, food, devotees, and so on. The challenge of hot bathing water in the mornings. And how once she and her partner were fortunate enough to get half a bucket of hot water when the power was out. It was a miracle; she had written and could only be Swamiji's grace. That's how the story ended. Well, I didn't completely disagree with her; finding hot water in the cold ashram winter was a miracle in the early years, but what about the grace that had saved her life?

When I had asked Tejas to detail his confession, I had no idea that he'd turn it into something so beautiful. It deeply touched my heart. I pray that Bhagavān's blessings rain love and joy upon him for times to come. For not everyone has the courage or the big heart to open up like he has.

Thank you, Tejas, for your goodness and kindness in penning this loving write-up. You've done me great justice (more than is true, perhaps) after the initial injustice. I'm only joking.

It's a human thing to judge. I do it all the time, and it is one of the things I've been working on myself. And it isn't just strangers, acquaintances, but family, friends, all judge us, and we judge them. It had been three years since my sannyasa, and I hadn't met my brother. I visited him in Dublin for a vacation. He was very happy to see me settled in a life that had brought me immense peace and happiness. Sunny is someone who has always stood by me and supported all my crazy decisions in life. A few days after I had made myself super comfy in his home, my brother said to me, 'I thought you'd be different now that you are a monk.'

He was referring in particular to my love for chocolate desserts and brownies that he'd see me devouring quite gluttonously. I couldn't pass a Starbucks without going in and packing a handful of brownies, only to return the next day to pick more.

My hand had stopped midway as I was about to bite into a caramel brownie.

'You haven't changed much,' he quipped.

But I had. Somehow his innocent remark had hit a spot. *Should I not be having these delectable desserts, or maybe not so many?*

I wanted to explain but all that came out was, 'Swamiji likes His disciples to be happy. He's lenient that way, so it's okay.'

I went to bed a little upset with myself, thinking maybe I'm being very un-monk-like, and I should show more restraint, especially when I so wanted to impress my little brother. For the last he had seen me, I was a pathetic mess chasing after a man to settle down with me.

A bit quiet and out of sorts, I wrote to Swamiji, an email, telling Him about what a great time I was having with my family. Since it was playing on my mind, somewhere I slipped in a line about my un-sanyasi-like behavior of having too many cakes and pastries.

When His response came, my eyes misted over. He had written:

> *Sadhviji, don't worry, it's Irish country after all. And you are indeed, the savior of desserts, their guardian angel. All the desserts look up to you, else they know they will go extinct.*

I had just sat there crying, reading and rereading these lines over and over, marveling at His compassion. Try as I may, I can never explain to someone how loving, non-judgmental and kind Swamiji is. If Vidya Swami was fond of music, then it was a Bose headset and a sound bar that Swamiji bought for him. If Vidu Swami liked to strap a watch around his wrist, then no ordinary watch would cut it, it had to be the latest Apple watch. It's how Swamiji is built, His happiness lies in the happiness of the other person. There's no mental or verbal sentencing for what each one likes to do or how they wish to live.

When people close to me keep piling me with chocolate cakes and I have one too many, He laughingly says, 'Bhikkuram, you are the custodian and patron saint of chocolate pastries. In the future, bakeries will hang your picture for your immense commitment to their cause.'

There's not a person I admire more than Him. Nothing you can do that'll make Him think less of you. Behind His simple affectionate manner and words is a vast consciousness that knows how each one is struggling and chipped at the corners. That everyone has quirks that they cling to, and in His kind-hearted way, He lets you, so that you may be happy. It's why, deep in my heart, this truth is set in stone: He'll always protect me, whether it's from an overdose of chocolate desserts or a lump in the arm.

The Founder

As the winds of Covid gained momentum and the world came to a standstill, Swamiji was fast at work. His vision of Sanatana Dharma's revival became His singular focus. There was no team back in 2020, but a single mind operating as a giant machine, assembling the big, small, and minutiae of the humongous Sadhana App endeavor. There were a million things that needed to be done to attain the perfection that you see in the app today. Swamiji's brilliance was matched only by His ability to execute the innumerable tasks, one by one until all the pieces fit in impeccably. He worked from dawn to dusk to midnight.

It was a tough year in more ways than one. Swamiji traveled alone in solitude, sans Vidya Swami and Vidu Swami due to the ban on international travel. Without His personal aides, food was a challenge. Of the two meager meals He ate in a day, lunch was sourced from a local place that served steamed rice and veggies. This was His lunch seven days a week. In the evening, after spending the whole day in front of the computer screen, frozen curry and chapatis were His dinner. A particularly painful time as well, as He'd experience excruciating pain in His knee many times in a day. This was a recurrent theme from the time He had healed a lady from an unknown neurological disorder a few years ago. To add to it all was the loud spike of Tinnitus that raged all day long.

Despite the many challenges in the physical environment, the work in the virtual world was far more demanding. The virtual worship of different deities required even a more elaborate set up than a temple in the real world.

The beautiful 3D and 2D idols, compelling temple environments, exteriors, every single piece of music to the more complex coding, software development, testing, UX designs, wireframes, UI, screen after screen, font after font, feature after feature, trailer, emblem, logo, audio recordings, every tiny detail before the human eye and beyond it was the labour of one person – Om Swami.

Every single pixel had passed through His eye. There's a cute expression Swamiji uses quite often when it comes to His coding and online venture, 'I like everything to be pixel-perfect.'

The cost of building the app was running into several hundreds and thousands of dollars as Swamiji put together an international team who charged in Euros and US dollars. 'It's important that Sanatana Dharma is shown in the glorious light that it deserves.'

The bulk of the funding came from Swamiji selling His stake in os.me to an incredibly kind soul. It is a different story that later when os.me was losing money, Swamiji bought it back and ended up owing the initial borrowing for the Sadhana App. A figure upwards of $1 million. 'I cannot bear the thought of anyone losing money when they work with me,' He often says.

Anyway, so one-and-a-half years later, pixel-perfect it was. By now Swamiji had worked on the app, day and night, not a penny was spared, or a dollar saved. All the income from His life-coaching too, was infused into engaging the finest and most talented artists from all over the world. He has since then stopped life-coaching completely.

I remember Vidya Swami and I'd often gasp in awe, when Swamiji showed us the latest works of Alex from Germany, or Loic and Immersive Garden in France and Edu and other designers in Spain. And then gasp in surprise for the money being paid out. The beauty of Swamiji's mind, His love for the Divine was on a course to recreate the glory of the Hindu Dharma as it once had been. We could all see that there was no stopping Him.

It seemed like an impossible and never-ending task at one point, as Swamiji was the employer and the employee. There was not another person to assist Him for eighteen continuous months. He was the whole and sole of this mammoth project. It was a project full of specialists and so the internal team was hired much later.

From Mar 2020 to Nov 2021, it was just Him working with numerous vendors. But thank God, for the remarkably passionate Vidu Swami, who negotiated with numerous Indian vendors for licensing rights and was utterly hands-on with the mountainous amount of translation involved. Also, let me just say this, managing Swamiji's diary is the most unenviable task. Every minute is accounted for. And yet, there was no rest, no sleep, no Sundays, no breaks, just a constant flow of work that kept Him up. It came to such a point that we actually gave up hope that things would ever go back to normal again.

And by normal, I meant a relaxed meal where afterwards Swamiji would make us laugh with His keen insights and divine humor. Exhausted and overworked as He was, He carried on with His ashram meetings, life coaching commitments and writing, nonetheless. It was a phase which I personally would never like to see Him go through again. The demands on His time and health were insane.

It wasn't until a few months before the launch of the Sadhana App that Vidya Swami and I insisted that Swamiji must take on people to help with the project.

The closer we got to the launch the more there was to do with wrapping up things. It was all ready, like a sprawling mansion, with doors, windows, décor everything done, only the final coat of the paint remained. We kept persisting that it was time to rope in a team to assist in the launch. Finally, when Swamiji's flawless execution had the app 90% ready, Priyanka Anand, the marvelous and formidable current CEO, was brought on-board.

She understood Swamiji's vision and possessed the same drive as Him to see it through. Bringing Priyanka in was a Godsend, for it allowed Swamiji's schedule to free up a bit. Under Priyanka's capable leadership the Vedic Sadhana Foundation(VSF) grew from two people to ten and on to its current strength of twenty-four full time staff.

This does not even include the more than forty contractors sourced through vendors who are being managed by the current COO, Vikram Shastry, working on various offerings of VSF. Swamiji's vision of Sadhana being a part of people's daily life has shaped beautifully. With the help of technology, He has revived an old-world order capable of transforming lives and shaping destinies. Today, Sadhana has become an indispensable part of the lives of over half a million people, who perform worship on the app daily. What a miracle, I say!

Onto The Next

Just when I thought, now we have Swamiji to ourselves for a while, He dropped the next bomb quite casually. One evening after dinner, Swamiji said to Vidya Swami and me quite casually, 'Think of a word that would make an exceptional domain name and handle.'

Oh no, what's Swamiji up to now?

You might think it funny but with Swamiji there's not a moment when His mind is not at work. He's someone who's constantly reflecting and indulging in the acquisition of more knowledge. So often Vidu Swami and Vidya Swami would mention some random piece of development in the world, a news item, a policy change and Swamiji would give them the entire history, the industry trend behind it.

His brain has this ability to store, possess and co-relate vast amounts of information that's impossible for an average person to even remember, let alone understand. The funny side to it was that Swamiji actually took immense delight at times in teasing Vidu Swami.

Swamiji would sometimes very casually slip in a song into the conversation, startling His dear and sincere disciple. It'd be the very song Vidu Swami had been humming in his head not moments ago. At time like this it's pure joy to see him squirming in his chair and saying, '*Guru Maharaj, aap toh sab jaante hain*, you know everything.'

I remember once we were travelling for an event, and I was sitting in the back seat with Vidya and Vidu Swami. Swamiji sat in the front in the hotel's car. The driver stopped at a red light, and I looked out to see two men on a bike to my left. They had similar helmets on, which were quite large for their heads. It somehow reminded me of a watermelon.

> *These guys look like two large watermelon-heads out for a ride on the bike.*

A smile had barely sprung to my lips, when Swamiji said from the front seat, 'Is it the season for watermelons yet?'

'Oh Swamiji, you are reading my mind.'

'I'm not,' He had replied adoringly.

If I started to recall all the moments and anecdotes being in Swamiji's holy presence, perhaps, this book will never see the light of the day.

Back to 2020, Swamiji was once again hard at work, in search of a domain name.

I had never met anyone who loved buying domain names for some distant day in the future when one might need it. It almost felt as if this was one of His favorite pastimes. By now I was used to Swamiji's nerdiness; He was and always will be among other things a software guy at heart.

Swamiji always liked to bounce off ideas and Vidya Swami and I were more than happy to be a part of Swamiji's yet another secret mission. Three days, and many permutations and combinations later, Wildr came into being. This became Swamiji's next pet project — a troll free social media platform that would allow for a deeper expression of one's self. He had started working on it at the same time as the Sadhana app, and internally it was codenamed 'Hummingbird'. But headed by the brilliant Vidit Drolia, the project was ready to graduate from internship and needed a public name now.

The beautiful and focused Melissa and software wizard Vidit (husband-wife duo) in the US, became the co-founders of this global enterprise. Soon Kunal Lunawat, a VC with excellent credentials, and degrees from Harvard and Yale, too joined the team. This project for the very first time made Swamiji hold meetings in public wearing His trademark all-black attire and not the traditional robes. 'It's just more convenient in every way,' He said. These were the same clothes Swamiji wore to the gym, but any day, it's the classiest gym look that I've ever seen.

Swamiji's simplicity of heart and clarity of thought wasn't dictated by the colour or design of His robe. He was a yogi at heart, detached yet forever striving to achieve excellence. With the same detachment He had given the reigns and day to day running of the Sadhana project to Priyanka Anand, as He focused His energies on building Wildr into a largely successful community. And time will tell of Wildr's success story and of its brilliant founder who envisioned it all along before anyone saw the merit in it.

Swamiji's ability to walk away once a venture turns profitable and fully functional is admirable beyond words. He hoards nothing, holds onto nothing.

Take for instance our beautiful ashram that has sprung up from a simple mud cottage with no running water and electricity into a marvel of solar panels, tall sadhak blocks, meditation hall, library, and a huge garden compound in practically six years as the real construction only started in 2016. Having given innumerable discourses in countless ashram events to keep it up and running, Swamiji gave the reigns of the ashram into the hands of the trustees and its day-to-day running into the capable care of Rajiv Mittal as administrator. Swamiji has not once looked back to ask about the ashram revenues or income. He continues to earn His living in the world through His own ventures rather than live off on the donations made by devotees.

As I was writing this book, I thought of asking Rajivji, (who's devotion to his Guru and dedication to the ashram is unquestionable and a great inspiration to me personally) about his experience of working and serving his Guru.

> *'In April 2015, we had the privilege of meeting Swamiji for the first time. Even today when I remember those three minutes spent in Swamiji's presence, my heart is filled with untold joy. His eloquent speech and humble manner instilled in me a great sense of belonging and surrender. Prior to Swamiji's darshan, I wasn't one to visit saints, mahatmas or storytellers, it was because of my wife Karuna that I had to reluctantly accompany her sometimes.*
>
> *'We didn't know much about Swamiji. We had only seen two-three videos of him on YouTube, which evoked in us a deep desire to see Swamiji in person and we made our*

way to the ashram. With his grace, as time passed by, my wife and I got the opportunity to participate in almost all the programs and festivals of the ashram. I felt the vastness and divinity of Swamiji, as we sat listening to his practical and profound answers to questions asked by devotees. Whether it was related to the occult or modern day living, his breadth of knowledge was phenomenal.

'Even today, it doesn't cease to amaze me how, with Swamiji's blessing, we found him on YouTube and reached the ashram located in such a remote place that we could not have imagined otherwise. My bond with Swamiji grew stronger over the years, as I received his immense love and grace. His guidance gave a new direction to my life. It is because of his presence, even the most critical and difficult situations in life don't bother me for long.

'Swamiji's tender and loving touch, to check my pulse, when I was ill once, touched the depths of my heart. He had left his important meetings to come and see me.

'During a discourse in January 2017, while announcing financial assistance to some children for education, Swamiji had said, 'Seeing the ashram, do not think that we have lack of resources, we can create a whole world if we want.'

'Swamiji's words made me feel as Arjuna must have felt seeing the great form of Lord Krishna. Many a time in his discourses, he's spoken of the importance of blessings. I understood the importance of blessings the other day, when, in return for my small help at Delhi Railway Station, an unknown elder blessed me that you should be successful in the work you are going for.

'It was surprising when that work, which could not be done in months, was done in a short time on that day. At

that time, I could not understand anything, but after listening to Swamiji's discourse, I understood the secret of blessings. My family and I are always under the grace of Swamiji, we always experience and realize it in some form or the other.

Thank you, is a very small word for Swamiji's grace, love and blessings. My one prayer to him is to always keep us under his shelter and that we learn to walk the path shown by him.

अपनी पनाह में हमें रखना, सीखें हम नेक राह पर चलना ॥

Just help us walk the noble path and keep us in your safe refuge.

Dasa Mahavidya

As the quiet months flew by, a sadhana of Mahakali was about to conclude for me. One afternoon, I woke up frightened by a dream. I narrated it to Swamiji, missing out on nothing. The setting was the same as our sanctum-sanctorum but instead of Sri Hari's *vigraha* there was a small black idol of Goddess Kali, clad in a red and gold sari. In my dream, I knelt at the steps of the sanctum to offer my pranams to Her. As I raised my head to look at Her face, those dark eyes of the *vigraha* flew open.

Seeing Her eyes black as the night struck great fear in me that She was angry with me. Those dark eyes startlingly clear flying open, stayed etched in my head even afterwards. I worshipped Mahakali in Her *sowmya swaroopa*, gentle form, so seeing Her like this was most disturbing. While growing up, my mother, although very loving, was quite strict with me. She had to be, as I was naughtier than most children and quite rebellious. It was a routine thing in the house for me to get a good beating. Back then, when I was growing up, this was just the culture.

When I started calling out to the Divine Mother, after my mamma's passing, I always sought the Goddess's love and gentle manner. The child in me longed for Her soft touch. I remember having a visualization where the Goddess fed me *dal-chawal*, lentils-rice, on Her royal dining table, like one would feed a toddler.

Seeing Maa Kali's flashing eyes had made me think of my childhood when mamma was upset with me over something I had done. I wanted the Divine Mother to love me, neither scold me nor be mad at me, just love me like She loved Lord Ganesha and Kartikeya. Often, in my visualization during my japa, both the children of the Divine Mother sat in Her lap on each side, and I on the ground holding on to Her.

It was so vivid and real to me that even in real life I imagined that they were my siblings. All this was running in my mind when I asked for Swamiji's reassurance. He sat unperturbed, serene like a beautiful lake on a winter afternoon hearing me babble.

'It's simply Maa Kali's way, Bhikkuram. She's the fearsome Kali after all. This is actually a blessing.'

'Yes, Swamiji, quite fearsome,' I swallowed hard.

On hearing this He laughed heartily. 'If you got scared just by seeing Her eyes, how are you going to do a longer sadhana of Her?'

Two months earlier, Swamiji had asked me while discussing my spiritual progress if there was a particular form I had an inclination to worship. And I blurted out Mahakali.

'I can get you to do the entire Mahadashavidya, Bhikkuram, it'd take several years, but you'd then be a sadhak par excellence... intuition, creativity, wisdom and siddhis, you name it, will come.'

But after Maa Kali's manifestation, I had a beautiful realization. I wasn't cut out for roughing it out with sadhanas. All I wanted was love, a whole lot of it, infinite and eternal. This wasn't my path. And what would I do with any siddhis etc.

anyway, Swamiji had every siddhi, one could possibly think of. As long as He was the only constant in my life and heart, I needed none of these things. And He'd always be there to watch out for me, for an eternity, of that I had no doubt.

On a more practical level, how could I ever hope to call out to Maa like Swamiji had. It was impossible. Where He had sat unmoving for twenty-two hours, I could barely sit still for twenty minutes.

All the time I spent by Sri Hari was spent dozing like a cat, and, with age, more like a cat-lady, either swaying forward or backward, hardly the posture of a sadhak, I'd say.

To be a sadhak like Swamiji requires the highest degree of mental strength and the highest purity of thought, both of which were missing in me. I also knew people, both devotees and non-devotees, who sat still for an hour or two in *dhyana* but even they seemed like pale replicas of Him. Their perfect posture, calm faces, and stirring manner of speaking were far from inspiring any kind of awe or devotion. The focus, discipline, and willingness to give up one's life to manifest the Divine Mother from a mantra and a Sri Yantra was something neither I nor anyone I knew could replicate.

Knowing my limitations and my desire for Sri Hari's love and worship eternally, I let Swamiji know, 'I think the Goddess Kali is beyond me. Instead, I'll pray to Lord Narayana, besides He's always smiling.' Swamiji chuckled adorably knowing how much Maa Kali had scared me.

As days passed, I soon realized that in seeking the company of both Bhagavān Narayana and Devi Lakshmi, alone, I was complete. Anything less or more wasn't for me. All other sentiments in me were an offshoot of the original *bhava*.

In the beginning, there were some silly notions, stemming from conditioning and what I had heard and seen, to have in my heart a love as pure and deep as Meera Bai for her Gopala. But that wasn't me. I learnt very early on that in bhakti, each one blooms differently. To follow the path of Meera Bai meant that I still had to be a grown-up. But deep in my heart, I was only a child longing for the divine couple's love. That one desire ran deeper than anything I had ever longed for. Their lap was the safest place in existence and their holy feet the playground where I knew no fear.

It was clear to me that Bhagavān and Maa were the root of my existence and, not one or the other but both. It's why worshipping Swamiji was effortless from the start, for He was a gentle mother to me when my mind refused to function like an adult. Where people saw anger and arrogance, He saw a distressed spirit. What others perceived as insolence and pride, He saw as unworldliness and fragility. In His saintliness, He only saw the good in every human being. His acceptance of my faults, imperfections, and the encouragement to be a better person brought about great transformation.

Much had changed since I first met Him after my mother's passing in 2013 but some things just hadn't. He still knew when my mind was caving in. And His words alone could bring me back from the brink of...as I wrote earlier in the book in Brahmachari Rishi's place, it could have easily been me. His emails had the same loving kindness and blessings today as they did then, when I was a stranger.

Until 2020, this and much more had transpired. I've shared as much as possible to pack in one book, not wanting to bombard you with too many stories, I've only chosen some relevant ones. To give you a glimpse into how the undefinable Karma and death can truly only be grasped and absorbed in one's consciousness by the grace of a holy one.

In a Nutshell

'Never turn your back to the ocean,' they say.

I heard somewhere that you can't turn your back to the power of the deep-sea, it'll drench you, catch you unaware, drown you when times are unfavorable. It pays to remember that time is never the same. The one force that acts as an anchor in choppy seas, the ship that pulls you to the shore is the grace of Bhagavān.

But Bhagavān is hard to find, they say; a Guru, on the other hand, a few mouse-clicks away. On YouTube and countless sites finding a Guru is as quick as finding a great sugar-free recipe. There are as many Gurus as the disillusioned lot that set out to find them.

The need to find meaning and respite from fate's relentless blows propels people on the quest for an enlightened being. There are, however, those accomplished few, who've absolutely no gripe from life. In that case, the presence of a Guru prepares you for any eventuality that the future might hold.

Pain, loss and failure are inevitable; it doesn't matter how much money you've in your account, or how content you are with life, this trio will come to you when the time is ripe.

Despite this biting reality, most folks are happy not to bother with spirituality, thinking and expressing themselves candidly, '*Kya yeh sadhu santo ke chakkaron mein padna,* what is the need to run after holy men.' They are right, there isn't, but one day there will be.

One day, surely, all that we've built, love, treasure, horde, and hold dear will be swallowed by a giant, unpredictable wave of life. In picking up the pieces of our lives is the realization that the only certainty there is – is of a greater force at work. A force that must be honored. What or who you have will be gone tomorrow; one way or the other, life will never be the same.

In this constantly changing life, if there's one constant, it is the presence of a Guru. His wisdom will never abandon you; it's ever-present. Whether the Guru is there in a physical body or not, his knowledge and grace are never far from a sincere disciple.

When people in the ashram bow to Swamiji's *padukas* in the temple in His absence, I wonder why bow to His *padukas* when He's standing right there in front of them. The great tradition and significance of the Guru's sacred *paduka* are not lost on me. The mind respects the devotional sentiment behind the gesture. It's the heart that sees no separation between the fair Lord, my Guru and the dark Lord, Sri Hari. In my head, it's akin to bowing to Swamiji's slippers when He's standing in front of me. I might not make sense, but then again, who can fathom the workings of anyone's mind, let alone their own? Each one worships a deity whom they aspire to be like.

In worshipping Swamiji, I've learnt to be independent, to be my own person. He has only ever encouraged me to develop my own conviction and rationale whilst praying to the divine. If my efforts have been twenty percent, His grace has been two thousand percent.

He was my mother's liberation, as He's mine. When He says a Guru isn't simply the end but the beginning of one's journey, He means for us to awaken the God within, to find enlightenment and lead a life of meaning and service.

He often says, 'Unique is the *rasa*, bliss, of *bhakti*, it cannot be found in the dry practice of *dhyana*, meditation. It's the ultimate union with the Supreme Soul.'

If anyone asked me to define *bhakti*, the first thing that comes to my mind is that, just as when a child is at school, or a man at work, the young mother or the new bride, while swamped with household chores, has only the thought of her darling on her mind, they are together in her heart. For togetherness is a mental state.

So is a *bhakta's* love for Bhagavān, their hearts remain entwined through the humdrum of daily life. There's no separation, merely a silent understanding that they are inseparable. That He'll come when I'll call. As Narayana came when little Dhruva chanted His holy names, Blue Krishna came at Draupadi's behest and the fierce Narsimha manifested from a pillar to save young Prahlad's life. And so is Swamiji to me, my only constant in this ever-changing world.

On this journey of self-realization, I seek no *siddhi* but the eternal love of Bhagavān and the Divine Mother. My only ask is that they grant me the power to love their creation, just as unequivocally. It'll surely happen with their grace one day.

My single most important discovery in seven years of sannyasa has been that the Sri Hari aarti is a potent hymn, a kind of secret hidden in plain sight. The fair Bhagavān, in flesh and blood, wrote it and the silent *vigraha* commanded in my dream that I sing it. It has brought my dormant dreams to come alive and an inexplicable bliss that comes from singing it.

It's not always the case but increasingly so, as I sing the aarti, my head starts to whirl like a leaf floating in a stream of joy. It's most pronounced when I wave the *chanwar* to Bhagavān. At this point, I'm the closest to Him. The magnetic pull of His presence is as if it's too much for my soul to bear.

It's difficult to keep my eyes open, and try as I may, the eyes close of their own volition. Such joy courses through the mind that it's an effort to keep myself from smiling like an idiot. Once, thinking that perhaps it's the brightness of the focus lights inside the sanctum that causes my eyes to shut close, I turned them off. Yet, the intoxicated feeling continued to hit me despite the dim lights.

It's strange that a song, an ode can numb the faculties of the mind with enchantment. On the days I'm able to immerse myself fully, a golden light illuminates my mind. The world starts to slip away like a dream; slip like an actual object about to clatter to the ground. The hypnotic pull of the *vigraha* is unlike anything I've ever experienced or known.

Even for a moment, I don't want you to think that this is a constant state. It isn't. But, it's also true that, on some days, the magnetic pull of Bhagavān's presence is akin to a physical sensation in the head. Just as when one smiles too much and the cheeks start to hurt, the constant flow of bliss from Sri Hari during aarti triggers a delightful ache at the fore and base of my head. On other days, it's Bhagavān's face that looms large. The adornments He wears, the *Shringaar*, the sandalwood around His face, the smile on His lips, it looms in front of my mind's eye. The nearer I'm to Him during the aarti, the more intense everything is.

I don't know what to make of it (or maybe I did make it all up) except that the beautiful dusky *vigraha*, is far more powerful and effervescent than you and I can imagine with our little minds. His divine play is so apparent in those moments, that I fear I might lose my balance or worse still faint. In all my 40 plus years I've never been the fainting kind, no matter what.

As Swamiji once said during a discourse that it's a different world outside and an altogether different realm that lies across the *garbgruha's* threshold.

'It's like when a tiny magnet is brought closer to a giant magnet. Nothing happens until you reach a certain point, at which moment the small magnet instantly slams into the bigger one.'

Maybe now my reluctance to bow to my Guru's *padukas* might make some sense; to me, He's standing in the inner sanctum at all times. Behind the tranquil eyes of Sri Hari, the playful smile and the wish-fulfilling, bliss-giving countenance, Swamiji is present at all times.

In a very key moment in the temple, Swamiji had once said, 'Sri Hari keeps Himself hidden in plain sight so well that, of the seven billion on the planet, only a handful find Him.'

Epilogue

As one of the temple priests at Sri Badrika Ashram, I lead a purposeful life serving Lord Sri Hari's *vigraha*, idol. The black stone idol is infused with both the masculine and feminine energy of my Bhagavān. Upon Swamiji's return from the Himalayas, having the divine vision of the Goddess and Lord Narayana, Swamiji lost no time in transferring many of His great *siddhis*, occult powers, to the idol.

In wanting to be fair, impartial, and unbound, He had entrusted the *vigraha* to be the keeper of His tapas, penance of not just this lifetime but innumerable ones before. Today, the idol appears more alive than a living, breathing human being, softly radiating peace and a fascination that'll keep pulling you back to the temple over and over again. As someone who dresses the *vigraha* daily, I live in constant awe of the changing *bhavas* of the Divine Mother and Bhagavān.

A mere woman, looking after the temple and the beautiful idol of Sri Hari, is somewhat unsettling for first-time visitors to the ashram. A visitor had once approached me with a few spiritual questions or so he thought.

'Why do you touch Bhagavān's face when you take off His garland in the evening. You touch it two to three times'

> *Last time I checked there was no crime in caressing the cheek of the one you love.*

I had just stared back at him, unable to formulate a reply. He had other interesting questions as well. 'Why did I close the door when I put Bhagavān to sleep, and was there any ritual attached to it? '

'Why couldn't he be allowed inside the sanctum?' In my response I had asked him if that was all he wanted to know. Were there no other questions pertaining to his spiritual practice or progress?

He shared that he was here to meditate as he had been following Swamiji for the past six months on YouTube. He wasn't impolite at all, but there was none of the regard usually shown to a person in an ochre robe or a woman.

I had also observed that while speaking to a male sannyasi he had a different approach. His questions were more refined, such as how he could meditate better, improve his practice and so on. I had wondered what had put my action under such scrutiny then. I don't really know, but it might have something to do with being a woman sannyasi.

I'll tell you what I said to him in a while. Before that I want to tell you a little story from around the time I was born, forty-three years ago. Sorry for the detour, trust me it'll make sense in the end.

The year was 1980 and my mother had a feeling before I was born that I was going to be a girl. The news of my birth was sent to my father and my grandmother (who was visiting us at that time). When my father received the news, he thought it best to first wrap up his game of gin rummy in the Army mess, while my grandmother caught up on her beauty sleep in the military hospital's cozy nursing quarters. No one was in a rush to see me or my mother.

Mamma had apprehensively waited for her husband and her mother-in-law to come see her newborn daughter. They didn't arrive until the next morning. Every once in a while, when Mamma told me this anecdote, her eyes would well up. She felt upset even after so many years.

So, while she waited for them, she prayed to her Ishta, deity Maa Durga, to watch out for us. And more importantly, when the time came to let her next child be a boy. She was quite devoted to the Divine Mother as most people in the Jammu-Kashmir belt are. She had lost her father, an Army-man, when she was five summers old. Her mother, a simple woman named Karma Devi, now lived with her sons and their wives, who were unkind to my mother, as she was somewhat of a stunning beauty even as a child.

Mamma had no one to really turn to except her new family. Hers was a love marriage and she worried that she might not be accepted or respected in her new home if she didn't have a son. Sounds familiar, even today, doesn't it? All these thoughts plagued her mind as she lay there on the hospital bed, alone, thinking of her fate and mine. The Divine Mother was her only refuge in those quiet moments.

The next morning the scene was quite different though, as my grandmother dashed in demanding to see her granddaughter and my father walked in as any beaming new father would. In the nurse's quarters where my grandma was resting, she overheard two nurses talking that to a Captain and Mrs. Tandon, a very beautiful baby was born the previous night. They wondered who the fair child had gone on, because the mother and father seemed quite wheatish to them. My grandma had chimed in, 'Oh she's gone on me. I'm the baby's grandmother.'

Doctor Guha, who had delivered me, was a renowned Army surgeon in Asia at that time, as my mother had told me on more than one occasion. And on meeting my father he had said, 'Captain Tandon, I've delivered hundreds of babies, but I haven't seen a more beautiful baby than your sweetie, here.' This is what doctors perhaps say to new parents, but my father had no idea.

Mamma said I was white like the inside of a coconut, with slits in place of eyes and a nose buried deep like a button. No eyebrows, not a hair on my head. I looked like a laughing baby Buddha, a very plump Chinese baby. The slits for eyes and no hair are about right but white-as-a-coconut, you should probably dismiss as my mother's wild motherly imagination.

Soon enough families from other wards came to see me, as word had travelled that there was a lovely baby in the family ward. Mamma said to me, 'Oh after that day your grandma never left my side. She loved the sight of all those people fussing over you.'

In less than a week of my birth, two things happened, my grandfather got an unexpected promotion and became a Joint Secretary in the UP government. Then came my father's promotion, a position that was coveted and utterly unexpected. According to mamma, he hadn't done too great in the recent training exam, and they were expecting a lesser position. The prized posting came as a big surprise to both my parents. Much to my mother's delight, the sudden boost in my grandpa and papa's fortune was attributed to my birth. Overnight, I became an auspicious baby; Doll was the nickname given to me.

I've no doubt that it was Mamma's prayers the Divine Mother had answered and Her grace that had turned the tide. At twenty-two, even though mamma had become a mother, she was still no more than a young girl. Going ahead, my grandma loved me dearly till she passed away when I was 13 and my father treated me as his princess and never denied me a thing as long as he was alive. No matter how unreasonable my demands, which they often were, they were always met, whatever be the cost. As for my mother, by now you know dear reader - a mother's love defies all laws of time and space. Her heart holds in itself no less than an ocean for the ones she loves.

If you ask me, somewhere, we are tough on our mothers, wives, daughters and sisters. Even in the most loving families, women's feelings are often ignored. So much is expected of them, but never do we give them the one thing they yearn for - our respect. They always have to prove their worth. They must project a certain image that gives credibility to the roles they play in our lives.

Why am I telling you all this? What does it have to do with the Divine? Everything, don't you think?

On meeting Swamiji for the first time, it didn't surprise me that Maa Jagdamba gave Him darshan in that little cave. He saw Her in everyone, women more so. I had thought to myself, there's a respect in His glance for our kind, a respectful glance, a deep appreciation for our intelligence, a care for our fragility. He gives us what we've always been owed – a respectful handling.

One might think that, beautiful as this attribute is, it's not a rare quality in the world. Yes, it isn't. What is rare though, is that this wasn't something Swamiji had seen or learnt. It was innate in Him. Matarani had shared a beautiful anecdote a while back.

Sunita, the lady who worked in Matarani's house, and whose son Swamiji had healed from leprosy (mentioned in *If Truth Be Told*), shared a special bond with Swamiji. Once, while doing the dishes, she had looked wistfully at the big water cooler in the house that was throwing cool air, 'This summer is harsher than most years. My son can't sleep because of the heat most nights, and neither can I.' An eleven-year-old Swamiji, who had been guzzling cold water didn't miss the sadness in her eyes.

That evening when Matarani came home, Swamiji ran to Matarani asking if she could pool some money to His savings, so He could buy a cooler for Sunita's home. He had three thousand rupees on Him and was short of two thousand. Matarani immediately agreed, marveling at her extraordinary child's ask.

The next morning, Swamiji was out of the house the whole day. He bought the cooler and spent the rest of the day getting it installed for the house help, so that the mother and son could sleep well that night. Swamiji's savings were all but gone and He had spent it without a moment's hesitation. It was His hard-earned money and not *shagun*, cash received as a gift from the elderly relatives.

Swamiji, even today, is like that eleven-year-old who gives each one, especially women, a thoughtful hearing when no one else does. The intelligence we possess and the trials in life that we've been through, is never hidden from Him. He's quick to put a cooler in our consciousness to calm the storms we may've been battling all alone. By His wisdom and grace countless lives have found new meaning, in circumstances that earlier seemed unbearable and unliveable.

In the last decade, under His awesome tutelage, my intellect and brain power have flourished like a cherry-blossom in spring. In 2018, He said to me, as I wrote poems after poem for Bhagavān like a woman crazed, 'It's a sign of Maa's grace, this unbridled creativity that one is unable to contain. It's why the sages of the yore, wrote scriptural texts after text during their life span. They just couldn't stop.'

For as long as I can remember, there's never been a moment when Swamiji has not put the interests of His disciples first. Having been so used to being regarded as an intelligent person, it comes sometimes as a rude shock when many visiting the ashram premises don't seem to see it that way. It's why when the visitor asked me why I touched Bhagavān's cheek, I felt confused. Would he have asked the same of a male sannyasi?

As a woman sannyasi, my behavior has to pass through a narrower lens. Only in Swamiji's eyes there's no distinction; in fact, being a woman in His presence only made Him more gracious and courteous towards us.

'I touch Bhagavān and Maa's cheek out of love,' I said to the visitor, 'Just as a child caresses her father and mother's face in affection.'

When he didn't reply, I asked, 'Do you have children? Do they not touch your cheeks lovingly?'

The visitor nodded in affirmation. But it hadn't made much of a difference to him. The truth is, to be close to Bhagavān, you've to be a child. There's no other way one can get close enough to them. In love, everything is permissible, in devotion, there is no need for permission; a child takes what he or she wants, do they not?

When Swamiji's grace ushered an era of temple service to Sri Hari in the summer of 2021, it didn't even occur to me that

I'd ever get a chance to do this beyond the summer. Raghu Swami's fractured leg and Vidya Swami's busy seva schedule brought this opportunity to my door.

I took each day as it came and dressed and fussed over Sri Hari knowing that I might not get the chance to be this close ever again. Having led an ordinary life in the world, the extraordinariness of standing near Sri Hari, the dark and gentle Bhagavān, was beyond my wildest imagination. How could I have ever hoped to have this seva forever? I had no such designs on Sri Hari, but the soul, perhaps, knew differently.

Though the road to this juncture has been long and full of toil, Swamiji's blessings have transformed me. All the spiritual progress I've made over the year is simply by flitting in and out of the Sanctum Sanctorum. In fact, Swamiji sometimes teases me that like the serpent, Vasuki, I'm forever coiled near Sri Hari, not letting myself out or anyone in.

It's rather funny because even as I type this, I'm parked on the steps of the Sanctum, with Sri Hari right in front of me. The truth is, the temple is my home, it's my address, my handle if you will - @home. Mornings you'll always find me there, and in the afternoons, for I can't tear myself away from them. By their side is the only place where my heart finds rest. It's a world where we are a tight-knit family, Sri Hari and I.

Being there, next to them, the petty unease of life, Swamiji's long solitude (getting even longer as the years pass), my mental challenges, everything feels alright.

To worship Swamiji and be in His service is my good fortune and it has come about after fifty-life times. These are the number of lives I've spent in search of my holy Guru, my Bhagavān, before I finally found Him in this birth. It has not been an instantaneous occurrence, rather a descent of a rivulet into an ocean, after travelling miles and miles of life's ragged terrain, picturesque plains, desert land and treacherous hills, before the rivulet disappears into itself - water into water. But even for water, finding water isn't easy, it doesn't always want to be found.

The same is true for my unassuming, down-to-earth master. His real self stays hidden behind a kind smile, wise words, back-breaking hard work, and perfectly timed jokes. You see, until you are in trouble, you will never really know the powerhouse that has been next to you all this while. He's on the outside a soft, tender, child of the Divine Mother; on the inside, however, He's the concentration of Shiva and the calm of Vishnu. The only constant in this ephemeral world—He's salvation itself.

In every drop of blood
in this inconsequential mass is You
I've not known You to be apart
as the Moon to the stars.

Your holy feet have walked
this heart a billion times
I rest in You
for where can I find
a home like yours.

O my Divine master
the holiness of life is You
the one true constant is You
in life and death
in the river of sorrows
that forever flow
You, like water, my Lord, are everywhere.

My humble obeisances in all prayers of the day in the holy and auspicious feet of the dark vigraha and the fair Lord, who are verily one.

जानकी नाथ सहाय करें जब।
कौन बिगाड़ करे नर तेरो ।।